CW00662499

A Unicorn in your Living-Room

A Unicorn in your Living-Room

A guide to Spiritual Illumination

Adela Simons

Copyright © 2014 Adela Simons

The moral right of the author has been asserted.

Apart from any fair dealing for the purposes of research or private study,
or criticism or review, as permitted under the Copyright, Designs and Patents
Act 1988, this publication may only be reproduced, stored or transmitted, in
any form or by any means, with the prior permission in writing of the
publishers, or in the case of reprographic reproduction in accordance with
the terms of licences issued by the Copyright Licensing Agency. Enquiries
concerning reproduction outside those terms should be sent to the publishers.

Front cover ©Josephine Wall
Used under license from Art Impressions
www.josephinewall.com

Matador
9 Priory Business Park
Kibworth Beauchamp
Leicestershire LE8 0RX, UK
Tel: (+44) 116 279 2299
Fax: (+44) 116 279 2277
Email: books@troubador.co.uk
Web: www.troubador.co.uk/matador

ISBN 978 1783064 649

British Library Cataloguing in Publication Data.
A catalogue record for this book is available from the British Library.

Typeset in Book Antiqua by Troubador Publishing Ltd
Printed and bound in the UK by TJ International, Padstow, Cornwall

Matador is an imprint of Troubador Publishing Ltd

*I dedicate this book to a very special
and unique soul…
You!*

PLEASE NOTE:

If you have any health issues, or other problems,
please consult your doctor or adviser before using any
of the information for yourself. Use the exercises and
meditations under their guidance and supervision.

In the event you use any of the information for
yourself, which is your choice, the author and
publisher assume no responsibility for your actions.

None of the material is intended to be an alternative
or substitute for traditional medical care, treatments or
other professional avice.

CHAPTER ONE

The Magic and Mystery of the Unicorns

It's said that:

'Once upon a time long, long ago unicorns walked the Earth.'

Those days of peace and purity are coming back, and the unicorns are returning to join us in great quantities… blessings of unicorns, in fact.

They are bringing their magic and mystery down to Earth from the Angelic Kingdom once again.

The unicorns are certainly alive and kicking!

We may still not be able to see them, but these magnificent and magical creatures are just around every corner, awaiting the call to your side, to join beside you on your spiritual path wherever it may be.

They are waiting to be invited into your life, and into the sacred space of your own living-room!

They have been with us since the very beginning of time, way back to the days of Great-Grandmother Earth, and the first years of creation of this beautiful planet of ours. They are part of our heritage and in our earliest spiritual memory.

It is in our deepest soul-memory that we remember the one-horned magical being, from ancient times which in everyday language we could call a 'horse with a horn'.

The unicorn.

It is often named as a mythological creature, which implies that it never actually existed. However, we are all blessed with freedom of choice, and so can decide for ourselves whether to believe that the unicorns were real creatures or mere figments of our imagination. Some of us do find it easier to acknowledge the existence of something if we have seen it personally, or at the very least seen a photograph of it.

Although I had never seen a kangaroo, I had every certainty that if I hopped on a plane, and flew across the world, that I would indeed see one, or several, and I did.

Here we go... I am being asked to stop immediately, and introduce you to Omega, my unicorn guide, mentor and narrator. He is rather impatient, and wants to speak!

He is the sacred, winged unicorn, who represents the brains, the beauty, the wisdom, the power and the glory of the Unicorn Kingdom.

Or so he says!

He really wants to communicate with us all, and so here he is, in full voice...

'So, excuse me for interrupting all this wonderful verbalising, but I thought that we had agreed that you were going to write about unicorns, who we are, where we come from, why we've reappeared and other important things!

Now you're talking about kangaroos!

Of course, I have the utmost respect for my antipodean friends.

However, if you were to describe an animal that hopped on its back legs, had a left hook like Mohammed Ali and kept its baby in a front pocket like an old-fashioned kitchen apron, you may well be excused for doubting its existence!

On the other hand, we, the unicorns have no such peculiarities.

I am a pure, white horse with a single horn, spiralling out of the centre of my forehead.

Pure and simple.

Do I exist indeed?

Let me tell you my story, and let's talk about the past, and see what you think.

The days when dinosaurs roamed the Earth and woolly mammoths walked the plains.

Where were we then?

Well, it has been told to me, by my ancestors and forefathers, that there have been unicorns since the very beginning of time.

So we are part and parcel of the furniture of the household of planet Earth, whether you believe in us or not.

It has even been told to me that in your Bible, the first book of Genesis used to tell the story of how God first gave Adam the task of naming every animal that he saw.

In some of the earliest translations the unicorn was the very first animal that he named.

That is why we are so proud, and it's said that when Adam and Eve left the paradise of the Garden of Eden

3

the unicorn went with them. This is the reason that people associate us with the original source of purity and innocence.

This stems from our place in history, in times gone by, when these fine qualities were commonplace.

Everyone and everything was light, pure and good.

We want these days of Heaven on Earth to return as soon as possible, and that's why we've come back to help speed things up a bit.

Do we exist?

How can you doubt it?'

Thank you to Omega.

The lineage of these celestial beings is of the highest order, and not to be underestimated. The unicorns exist on a different vibrational frequency to ourselves, and that is why we are unable to see them in a normal everyday way.

They are of the angelic realms, and subsequently of a very high energy, like the angels and archangels. If we want the unicorns in our lives then we have to try to be as focused as possible on the good in everyone, and 'raise our game' to try to meet their very high standards!

Talking of high standards, they have pride of place on the British Coat of Arms, supporting the royal shield with their supposed arch enemy, the lion.

In fact, they were depicted on the front page of every wedding service sheet of Kate Middleton and Prince William.

A Royal seal of approval, no less.

Talking of royal seals of approval, certain food

products are marked with the British Coat of Arms and the words 'By appointment to her Majesty the Queen', and so there is the unicorn, again in pride of place…in your fridge!

On every jar of Colman's English mustard, and HP Sauce, for example, there is a unicorn.

Once you start to look they are indeed everywhere.

They have these royal connections indeed, but as well as this there are the many wonderful stories, ancient tapestries, and pictures that exist of this magical creature in all cultures and continents.

The unicorn is probably the most beautiful, sacred, magical and mysterious of all the animals, past and present, in the Universe.

They also have many religious associations. They were mentioned in the original 1611 edition of the King James Bible. In Isaiah 34, verse 7, it read:

'And the unicorns shall come down with them.'

It is an absolute travesty that every mention of a 'unicorn' in this Bible was then apparently substituted with the words 'wild ox'.

A very unfortunate translation, to say the very least!

'Wild ox, indeed! Huh!'

Guess who?

Perhaps here I should try to describe how Omega appears to me, you may 'see' him differently. Here goes…

Omega is a very handsome unicorn, majestic in stature, regal in pose, strong in attitude, gentle but powerful by nature, soft in the eye, with a pure white body with golden hooves and wings. His horn is straight and true, like a spiral of carved ivory, and nearly 2 feet long. He holds his head high, with a tilt to the side. It has to be said, he has rather an 'aloof' air about him. He is telling me here that his look is more quizzical than snooty!

Just like the hummingbird the winged unicorns, like Omega, can fly in any direction – up, down, backward, forwards, or even hover.

He can fly slowly, or at breakneck speed.

He can walk beside you, if you need to proceed with care and caution.

He is supremely adaptable, intuitive, telepathic and empathic to the highest degree.

Humour is a great quality he has in abundance, not of the slapstick variety, but rather on the sophisticated side!

He represents Pure Love, Pure Light and is a Pure Delight to work with, as are all the Angelic Kingdom of angels, archangels and unicorns.

Quite an amazing celestial creature, by anyone's standards.

We are very lucky to be graced with his presence. He's saying that, of course!

Whether you believe that they are purely figments of imagination, that they are fairy tale creatures, or that they actually lived in times gone by, and that they have returned with the angels *now*, the common theme is that they are most definitely magical, mysterious and are here to help us once again.

According to legend they cannot be tamed or caught, but who would want to anyway.

Freedom is one of the major qualities that they bring to us. We all have the freedom of choice, and can choose whether we want to move forward, stay put or move on.

We always have a choice, and the unicorns bring us to recognise that freedom.

They also represent total purity, courage, compassion, are dignified and proud in stature, and bring love into our lives.

The unicorn is a symbol of the soul, and brings us the glorious gifts of the soul such as love, wisdom, freedom and understanding.

But let this story begin, this story of love and healing, of support and guidance from the Angelic Kingdom, from the unicorns themselves, as they return to help us on our journey towards peace on Earth, and the Golden Age which is drawing ever closer. Many believe that it was indeed the Winter Solstice of 2012 that opened the door to bring the mysteries into the light and to begin the final process of our soul Ascension into the Fifth Dimension.

This book takes us on this magical journey of soul illumination and transformation.

The ability to grow, develop and move on is in all of us. We need to feel secure, loved and protected to face up to the challenge.

We need to feel valued for what we are in order to be able to confront change, and move onwards.

Sometimes, we come to a crossroads in our life, the

7

direction to follow is unclear, maybe confusing, and sometimes someone or something appears to help us choose which way to go in our lives.

Then, the decisions are easier, and the path reveals itself in unexpected and wonderful ways.

Life continues anew, different challenges, new beginnings, the growth of 'self' nearer to the Light, nearer to the Divine purpose of our life.

Challenges afresh, rewards for the route chosen, some disappointments and upsets when the road becomes rocky, or feels unsafe, and the going gets tough.

At these times we look for our spiritual friends to gently guide us, support us, love us and value our journey.

These are our special friends, the very important ones that we know we can rely on whenever and for whatever we need them.

Yes, the unicorns are some of these special spiritual friends.

A blessing indeed.

The journey does not have to be half way up a mountain in Tibet, but can be deep into the sacred space of your own living-room!

It is a journey *within*. Wherever you happen to be.

A journey to *find yourself*...to find the source of the inner light within you, your SOUL.

Who you are.

What you want and

What you are here on Earth to do.

The journey to enlightenment and illumination is for

your soul, and to open your heart to the love that surpasses all others.

Follow your heart

It will lead you in the right direction.

On your road, the going may get tough, the road may be rocky.

Bereavement, redundancy, loss, abandonment, illness, disability etc.

These are the times we need our spiritual friends, to support us with *love*, and help us on our way again.

The unicorns are part of this support group.

They will give us the pure, undiluted power and energy to *move on*, in LOVE and LIGHT.

They will show us the way, and lead us forward again.

NEVER UNDERESTIMATE A UNICORN!

They can be a valuable tool in the 'tool-box' for your spiritual journey for occasional support, and help at times of need.

'Tool in your tool-box, indeed!

Charming! I've been described in many ways, but never in such a mundane manner before!'…that's Omega interjecting.

Alternatively, they can be a <u>MAJOR</u> part of your journey, and be there for you 24/7.

The pace may sometimes be fast, but always in the right direction, towards purification and enlightenment.

Your soul journey can be faster, and more fun on board a unicorn, or with a unicorn on board, and you will certainly never be bored!

In some stories the unicorns are described as aloof, or even standoffish, and seem to be very particular about how they are perceived, and who they decide warrants their help and healing.

Here's our regal friend Omega again, he speaks…

'What do you expect? The human race had it all, in the old and ancient days, love for each other, care of the natural world, respect for the Animal Kingdom and trust in each other.

Supporting, encouraging and inspiring the underdog and rejoicing and sharing in the achievements of others.

What went wrong?

The power, and abuse of power, tainted and destroyed the balance and harmony of those early days in Atlantis and the like.

We, the unicorns, need to be sure that the humans, who call on us for our help and healing energies in these dark and dismal days, are pure of heart, and trying to do their best for the planet and for the survival of humanity.

We are delighted to bring in our Love and Light to those who are aspiring to reach for the stars, and lift the human consciousness back up to the heights to which it is capable.

For these people we bring our energies in abundance to enlighten, empower and energize… those who need help and support to raise their vibrations to their full Divine potential.

Call on us when you need to be strong in a situation.

Call on us if you are trying to live a life without drugs, alcohol, overwork, over-eating or other harmful activities.

Call on us for our healing powers, and gifts of purity and compassion, and let us bring beauty into your life, and the courage and stamina to change your life around.

Call on us if you are battling with negative thoughts: anger, fear, pain, doubts and confusions; let us bring clarity and positivity into your life.

We are Divine creatures from the angelic realms, and we want to help you, and when you are ready to call us into your lives, we will respond with love, strength, purity and beauty and will bring magical healing and positive energy into your lives.

We are, it's said, magnificent, magical white beings and we are now returning to Earth in large numbers to help bring PEACE and PURITY to humanity, and your planet.

We are here for YOU.'

These are the wise words given to me by Omega.

He is the brains and the beauty, the wisdom, and represents the power and the glory of the Unicorn Kingdom. He just wanted me to repeat that again!

It appears that this story of healing, support, humour, love and guidance will be an interesting mix of unicorn narration and human endeavour!

11

We've, hopefully, written it in a form which can promote healing, and at times may touch you and resonate at the deepest level of your soul.

There is something here for everyone; be you a sleeping soul, a lost, lingering or lazy soul or if you are already an enlightened master soul!

Harnessing the unconditional love and power of the Unicorn Kingdom also ensures a fast and magical journey for you towards illumination and nearer to the Ascension into the Fifth Dimension of the Golden Age of Heaven on Earth.

Let the magic continue… and remember wherever you find unicorns you can guarantee that angels are close by.

EXERCISE ONE

Introducing yourself to the unicorns.
Keeping a journal.

Please consider buying a notebook, or a beautiful journal, whichever you can afford.

This can be your own special and sacred written record of your journey with the unicorns as you walk with them through this book.

Your guardian angel will be at your side throughout, loving and supporting you, as always.

This is not an exercise in the use of the correct grammar or spelling. This is *your* journal, for your eyes only!

(Therefore, please be aware of keeping this journal in a safe and secure place.)

Writing down your thoughts and feelings is a very healing, and therapeutic exercise. It is also a powerful method of becoming more self-aware and understanding yourself.

Using your journal is simplicity itself…

Keep your journal close at hand as you read this book.

If any passage or word touches you, or brings any negative thoughts etc. to the surface, then that is the moment to try to hold on to that thought or feeling in your mind until you've picked up your pen. Write down exactly what it is that you're feeling or thinking. Hopefully, you may have lots of wonderful magical moments with the Angelic Kingdom of angels, archangels and unicorns to write about too! This may be a healing experience, a deep connection, a clarification on a problem, or a positive insight into yourself and your soul lessons. Putting your thoughts and feelings down on paper can be very therapeutic, and help you to understand yourself better.

You can also use this journal for the exercises at the end of each chapter.

Before you start this amazing journey of self-discovery, healing and learning it may be appropriate for you to dedicate this journal, and its contents to your unicorn and angel friends.

A Dedication and Intention

Simply relax, breathe deeply, close your eyes, and mentally ask that you be supported and guided to greater wisdom.

Introduce yourself, and still in a relaxed state of mind, note down any feelings you may have at this point.

If you are really blessed you may sense a warm energy, or a colour or even a name of your unicorn guide.

Do not be disappointed if nothing seems to happen, it's early days!

Whatever may have happened or not happened please write an entry in your journal.

I promise you that when you revisit this journal in days or years to come it will resonate with your soul, and bring you joy and pleasure.

It is so very interesting to reread these early notes as you progress further on your journey to find and connect with the unicorns and other members of the Angelic Kingdom.

This is the beginning of a new and honest dialogue with yourself, your inner wisdom, higher consciousness, the very wise person within or whatever else you like to call yourself!

CHAPTER TWO

Unicorns, Angels and The Light

What exactly will a unicorn bring into my life?
How can I bring a unicorn into my living-room?!

The unicorns are very high-energy beings, and because of this will be drawn to individuals and groups where the energetic vibrations are also high. If *you* feel drawn to the unicorns, and want to invite them into *your* life, then this is YOU!

Unicorns are just like people in one regard, and that is in that no two are the same, just like fingerprints or a zebra's stripes.

We are each special, unique and a one-off!

The Unicorn Kingdom is no different. They may be any size, colour, shape, and even with or without wings. Their characters and personalities are also infinitely variable.

Magically, we seem to attract the perfect unicorn for ourselves that we need at any particular time. If we are deeply sad we will probably connect with a tender and compassionate unicorn.

If we are lacking motivation, and feel stuck in some way we will probably attract a unicorn with a positive attitude who may well give us a spiritual 'kick up the backside' to encourage us to move forward!

Omega is telling me here to tell you what a very fine, upstanding, majestic, and powerful example he is of the Unicorn Kingdom.

He is also saying with a twinkle in his regal eye that modesty has never been his strong point!

They are from the angelic realms, and so it's highly likely that when we prepare to welcome the unicorns into our lives, that the angels will come along too.

However much of an individual each unicorn is, they all share these most amazing qualities and bring us the gifts of the Angelic Kingdom, which include:

- unconditional love
- guidance
- purification
- protection
- courage
- joy
- wisdom
- peace
- forgiveness and innocence, to name but a few.

The unicorn also encapsulates all the fine qualities of the horse, which as a power animal will bring along all these additional advantages into your life as well:

- strength
- reliability

- mobility
- power
- freedom and
- friendship, to name but a few!

Happily with these spiritual horses, the unicorns, there are no feeding costs, no livery charges, no vet's bills, exercise is definitely not required and certainly there is no mess to clear up!

So it's all positive…just as you would expect.

This magical mixture then has the unique blend of ingredients that only the actual unicorn can bring, as follows… all conveniently beginning with the letter 'p'.

- PURITY
- PEACE
- PROTECTION
- POWER
- POTENTIAL
- POSITIVITY
- PASSION and
- PURPOSE

There is still more. The list is almost endless.

We now have to provide the extra ingredients, to enhance this powerful combination, the truly exceptional qualities which only a unicorn embodies, which add to this remarkable mixture…all conveniently beginning with the letter 'm'.

- MAGIC
- MYSTERY
- MAJESTY
- MASTER-HEALING and
- MIRACLES

What a heavenly horse this unicorn really is…it almost defies description. Words cannot do justice to this stunning, spiritual steed!

This is beyond doubt a wondrous creature like no other.

When you embrace the energy of the unicorn, and ask them into your life expect…

- Whoosh! and Wow! Moments and
- 'Expect the Unexpected'

These two expressions, for me, characterize the forms that unicorn energy may well appear in your life.

A Whoosh! And Wow! Moment is an exciting mixture of amazement, high-energy, magical, breath-taking, jaw-dropping, high-octane wonderment!

Expect the Unexpected sums up the sheer unusual, eccentric, quirky and highly unpredictable nature of unicorn energy in action!

There is nothing mundane, nondescript, ordinary or lacklustre about our unicorn friends.

All these unique qualities are magically bonded together to combine all the beautiful, ethereal angelic qualities with the fine, strong characteristics of the horse to produce the marvellous and most fabulous being of the Angelic Kingdom, the Unicorn.

*This is the magical being that **you** can connect with, and ask into your life and into the everyday world of your living-room!*

How can I connect with a unicorn?

How can I sense the presence of a unicorn?

Once you have started to try to communicate with unicorns and the Angelic Kingdom they will find ways to contact you, or validate their presence.

The connection with these beautiful beings will touch you, and enhance your life in ways you could never imagine.

The unicorns are with us, and will alert us to their presence in any way they can, however unexpected or unusual.

On a personal note, I was thinking about the wonderful way the unicorns had stampeded into my life (but that's another story!). I was mentally questioning myself about what had happened, and deciding if it was all in my active imagination, or not!

I was walking through the local hospital reception area, at the time, and I noticed a young mum standing by her pushchair. She was wearing a sleeveless shirt, and was well adorned with an assortment of tattoos. I was immediately transfixed by a picture of a magnificent unicorn-head on her upper arm.

I took the precautionary decision not to stare and to look away quite quickly, but nevertheless, I got the message!

So, how do we communicate with them?

Is it very difficult, and complicated?

Our friend, Omega, wants to say a few words, straight from the horse's mouth, as it were!

'Very amusing, my dear, how very hilarious!

Personally speaking, I find it most endearing and very encouraging if someone wants to speak to me, that they just do it.

If you want to light candles, burn aromatic oils and play melodic music then that is truly wonderful, even if not at all necessary, on my behalf.

I respond to peace, love and harmony.

If you can try to relax, clear your thoughts and open up your heart, and call on myself, and the angels, and other unicorns for help, healing, guidance, support, courage or whatever quality you need to help either yourself or others at the moment.

Just quietly, mentally ask us into your life, and we'll be there, in your living-room, in a flash.

Simple as that!'

Thank you Omega.

It really is that easy. Talking about them, reading this book, even just thinking about the unicorns will inevitably draw them even closer.

They may come to you with a piece of music which touches your soul, or with a beautiful sunset which brings a tear to your eye.

On our spiritual journey there will be signposts, and synchronistic events along the way.

We must have our eyes open and look out for them…
Signs! Signs! Signs!

Be on the lookout for any indications, validations or signposts to follow.

Expect the unexpected when the unicorns are about.

They are not called magical beings without good reason.

What exactly are the signs likely to be?

On a personal note, I had read that seeing a white feather can be a sign that an angel or a unicorn has visited you.

I was thinking to myself that I hadn't seen any white feathers, even a tiny one!

The next day, I'm looking out of my window, and there on my garden wall is…an exquisite, totally pure white peacock.

I learned my lesson, in a rather majestic style.

I have never seen such a magnificent, splendid, more beautiful sight in my whole life.

It was absolutely stunning, and although I really struggled to believe my eyes, my neighbours and I enjoyed the presence of this regal, angelic bird every day for the next week.

White feathers in absolute abundance!

Now that's what I call a SIGN…

A supreme validation for me, and a truly amazing indication that all was well.

When unicorns share your spiritual journey expect this sort of Whoosh! And Wow! moment.

(The peacock had obviously been on its own adventure, escaped its enclosure, and avoided recapture for just over a week. I can still hear its eerie and haunting call sometimes, which reminds me of its existence, and its powerful message for me, which came just when I needed it.)

Signs may come in smaller ways, a song you hear with words which are the answer to a question you have been seeking, an unexpected telephone call from an old friend you had been thinking about, a book which jumps off the shelf to be read or a strange feeling you have which leads to a welcome surprise.

It could be a beautiful white feather, of course!

Omega wants to talk to us again,

'**If you are a Lightworker, such as a healer, teacher, counsellor, nurse or the like, call on us always, and we are at your side in a flash of light.**

If you are a dustbin man and help an old lady with her rubbish, you too are a Lightworker.

If you are unemployed and smiled at the lady in the benefit queue when she broke down in tears, you too are a Lightworker.

If you are depressed, abused, in pain, disabled, discriminated against, poor, weak, troubled, anxious, alcohol or drug dependant you can call on us for help.

You too are very special.

You too are unique, and bring your own beautiful soul into this world.

You too can be a Lightworker.

Talk to us, we will listen, and then just await the signs which we will show you to help you to understand and communicate with us.

Be patient, and trust yourself.

We're not far away, and are waiting to come to your side.'

Thank you, Omega.

One thing leads to another.

Miracles CAN happen!

Particularly when the unicorns are involved.

What exactly is a Lightworker?

Lightworkers are those human beings who are drawn to help and heal others in many different ways for the benefit of all humanity.

This book is a universal book of light to reach both those souls seeking the light and those already of the light or Lightworkers.

The angelic realms will be drawn to all Lightworkers, but are equally drawn to those that are struggling with the darker side of life as well!

The following affirmation is inspired by the archangels, those angels who work at the highest frequency of Love and Light.

If you feel called upon to be a teacher, a nurse, a secretary, or a healer,

Whatever you choose

Do it with a PASSION, this is the energy of the soul,

And your Light will shine, inspire and help others.

A teacher may be the person that a frightened, abused child decides to trust and disclose the horrors of their life.

Every job has opportunities to make a difference in this world.

All potential healers.

YOU do make a difference.

Every time someone connects with an angel, or talks about a unicorn, or does a good deed, or helps someone in distress with a kindly word or a warm smile, a small spark lights up the planet.

Another light goes on in the darkness.

Each light counts.

All these small lights help bring healing to mankind.

Healing to the planet.

Imagine, in an enormous building even one small candle makes a difference.

One small light in the darkness changes everything for the better.

A glimmer of hope.

A small ray of light in the darkness may be the light at the end of the tunnel to guide a lost soul back to the love of the Light side.

Yes, YOU do make a difference.

Let your light shine.

Never underestimate your own special and unique input into the Light of the world.

You count, and

Yes, YOU do make a difference.

Once the lines of communication are opened with the unicorn and the Angelic Kingdom you may well receive powerful messages of support, love and guidance, like this one.

This is your time, as a spiritual being on your human journey, and you can ask them into your life at any time.

If your intentions are pure, and you genuinely want to follow the spiritual path, to the Light and illumination then it's time to call in the unicorns.

The unicorns will lead you, guide you, take you, find opportunities for you and put people in your path that will help you on your journey.

The unicorns are the celestial catalysts that speed up and accelerate your journey in their own magical and mysterious ways.

Hang on in there.

This is spiritual alchemy at work, with the master magicians...the unicorns.

They can bring peace and purity to you, which will help you towards healing and enlightenment.

Improving how you feel about yourself, in turn automatically helps others,

I.e. The people in your life, partner, children, colleagues, neighbours and more.

All those close to you can benefit from your healing, and the positive energies can spread outwards to others, like a web of light.

Light is one of the two most powerful spiritual energies.

LOVE and LIGHT is the powerful pair!

The Angelic Kingdom of angels, archangels and unicorns are all surrounded by a powerful light. This is where the halo-effect originates in many paintings, stained-glass windows etc. around the heads of celestial beings.

It is called the aura, which is our own light of different colour, quality, and quantity of our own projected energy-field, which varies depending on our mood or frame of mind!

This is the Divine power of pure, genuine UNCONDITIONAL LOVE at work.

The archangel that, I feel, is the 'leading light' at the moment is ARCHANGEL URIEL.

The meaning of Uriel is 'The Light of God' and 'The Light and Fire of the Divine'.

He is the archangel who has been 'waiting in the wings', and now is coming to centre stage as the Archangel of Light, who is the overseer of all the Alighting Angels and the Sacred Winged Unicorns who are gathering together to bring us back to the days of Heaven on Earth.

Meanwhile, bring them into your life (and your living room!) and they will add a new dimension to your existence, and bring you untold gifts of miracles and magic!

So let the magic continue, and the Light shine...

A Meditation with Omega

"To communicate with your own unicorn"

There is one ancient method of trying to communicate with your Higher Self, and your spiritual source or soul. This is called meditation.

Meditation is also a wonderful method to visualize, and to encourage your connection with the Angelic Kingdom, unicorns included!

There are many and varied books on the subject of meditation, the techniques and the methods to use.

Meditation is a powerful healing device on all levels of being:

I.e. the physical, mental, emotional and the spiritual.

The following meditation is quite simple and straightforward.

If you wish to develop this technique further there are usually evening classes available locally.

(Before you start this meditation please ensure that you are not on any medication or have any emotional or mental health issues which would make it an unsuitable time for you to do this exercise. If you are in any doubt it would be sensible for you to check with your doctor first.)

I now hand over to our unicorn friend Omega, who will help us to prepare for this meditation.

'Welcome friends to the opportunity to relax, and still your mind, and open your heart, in perfect peace and safety, surrounded and protected by your unicorn and angel friends.

Join me on this journey of love and healing.

Let us feel the freedom and release from earthly worries and concerns, and move quietly and gently in our meditative state to the beauty, and purity, and innocence of the Higher Self, in the Great Silence.

Let us begin by choosing a time when we will not be disturbed, and find a place either indoors or a quiet seat in your garden where you feel safe and secure, comfortable and relaxed.

Close your eyes, and focus on your breathing, nice and slowly and deeply.

Relax your body, drop your shoulders, and feel as if you haven't a care in the world, and as if your whole body is fluid and melting into the earth.

Feel your feet touching the ground, and try to think of roots growing out of the soles of your feet, and pushing down into Mother Earth, anchoring you safely. You are now grounded, down to earth and in touch with reality, safe and secure in every way.

Think about your breathing again.

Breathe in slowly and naturally five times.

Allow any thoughts that come into your head to float away and come back to your breathing.

When you exhale try to imagine all the tensions, toxins, and any stressful feelings you may have draining down the roots from your feet, and out and away to be released in Mother Earth, where they will be recycled.

Reinforce this by releasing a deep sigh on the out breath.

Let it all go.

As you inhale try to visualise the beautiful, healing light of the Angelic and Unicorn Kingdom filling your body with all the Love and Light you need.

Relax and trust me, you are safe, and enfolded in the loving embrace of angel wings, and have the strength and compassion of the unicorns with you.

When you feel ready, put your hand on your heart, sense the connection with your inner light, your Divine centre, and breathe deeply.

Enjoy the magical feelings of love and security washing over you, and filling you with peace and tranquillity.

Let your body, and mind, and soul rejoice in this beautiful, sacred space you have created for yourself.

Remember this is somewhere you can return to at any time.

It is yours forever. Whenever you desire this place, it is yours. Only for you.

The special and unique person that you are.

Now, if you feel ready, you can call on your angel and unicorn friends and invite them to join you.

Ask them to draw closer, and open your heart to them.

They are so warm and gentle, and fill you with tenderness, and you feel enveloped with feelings of harmony, joy and wellbeing.

Stay in this moment, relaxed and at one with the world.

We are all different, and will each have a unique experience.

Maybe a unicorn will come quietly by your side,

Your guardian angel may touch you with an angel feather,

You may feel very emotional and full of peace,

You may be surrounded with intense vibrant swirling colours,

You may feel as if you are floating on a cloud,

You may hear voices, singing, or music playing,

You may not see or feel anything at all,

Do not worry, or be concerned,

Try to enjoy this special, sacred and peaceful time,

Relax and understand that you will feel what is right for you at this time.

Trust and believe in yourself.

When you feel ready to come back to waking consciousness, gently become aware of your body, wriggle your toes and have a little stretch, come back to normal breathing.

Feel your feet.

Give mental thanks to those who have helped you in your meditation, your angels and unicorn friends.

Time now to mentally say goodbye to me, Omega, until the next time.

Open your eyes, and return to your surroundings.'

Thank you to Omega for his input, and this beautiful meditation.

It is important to ensure at this point that you are fully grounded, and it is advisable to wash your hands, and have a glass of water before continuing.

Maybe even put the kettle on for a nice cup of tea.

You deserve it!

How are you feeling?

Did you see a unicorn?

Were you able to relax?

Now, at the end of this first meditation session it is very useful to record and write down any feelings, or experiences in your journal.

You are now becoming closer to the Angelic Kingdom, and starting to open the door of communication between the earth plane, and the heavenly realms.

Magical!

Don't worry if you didn't feel or sense anything.

We are all different, and all come to the boil at different times.

It's still a good idea to write an entry in your journal, however short it may be.

CHAPTER THREE

Unicorns as magical Master-Healers

The unicorns are master-healers. It is because they are from a higher spiritual dimension than ourselves that their healing is also at a higher frequency. The energies that the Unicorn Kingdom can bring into our lives are magical, mystical, intensely powerful and 100% pure.

It is because of this positive combination of high-octane energy and healing-power that miracles are well within the realms of possibility when the unicorns are around and about!

What exactly is healing?

In a spiritual sense 'healing' is when positive energy is channelled or guided into someone, which brings them into a state of peace, calm and balance. This spiritual healing may bring healing at the deep level of the soul, promoting peace of mind, and can also encourage physical and emotional well-being.

There are many different sorts of healing which are based on spiritual energy transference, such as spiritual healing, Reiki, crystal healing and healing with colour and crystals.

Spiritual healing is an ancient therapy. The first recorded spiritual healer-priest was Imhotep, who was healing in Egypt in 2900 B.C., nearly 5000 years ago. Not exactly a new-age therapy!

In a nutshell, spiritual healing works almost solely with channelled energy.

Reiki uses energy with ancient healing symbols, crystal healing uses energy and crystals (selected appropriately) and healing with colour uses energy with a selected colour/s suitable for the recipient. Crystals, colours and symbols all have their own different energies. A healer using these particular methods will be trained to use the appropriate crystal, colour or symbol to intensify and direct the healing energy to a specific area during the healing session.

When I qualified as a spiritual healer I was asked by a friend and colleague whether I had asked the angels to help me with my healings.

'Can I do that?' I asked.

I was thinking curiously, 'Me?'

I was reassured that they really do want to help, but that we must always 'ask' them.

So I did, ask them, and they did, help me!

I work with a 'hands-off' method, but my clients were immediately telling me that they could feel the touch of extra hands at work. Some could feel a cool breeze around them, some saw swirls of colour, or an angel's wing, some felt a warm presence, some saw fluttering wings, and I soon realised that I was not working alone.

It is a privilege and a beautiful experience to be able to work with the Angelic Kingdom in this way.

All we need to do is 'ASK', and, believe me, they come.

Yes, this is YOU!

What can the unicorns do to help with healing?

I discovered that all the Angelic Kingdom of angels, archangels and unicorns are extremely happy to help with healings, and also any other spiritual pursuits.

Unicorn energy is *very* special.

They are very adaptable, and they will adjust their speed to travel at the rate which we determine.

If we need to move forward, but are frightened or reluctant in some way then the unicorns will *walk* beside us.

If we are ready to travel to the next stage of our journey rather faster, then they will travel beside us with a gentle *trot*, a fast *canter* or if we are prepared for it…a full-out *GALLOP* with all four of their golden hooves off the ground!

We will learn how to harness the unicorn's power for self-healing, and in turn for the benefit of all mankind. This is a spiritual energy like no other, and is indeed a blessing.

A group of unicorns is in fact called a blessing.

They will help us, whatever spiritual level we are at, to progress to the very *best* of our personal potential. They are strong, and sure-footed, and they see the pitfalls and temptations on our spiritual road, and they will carry us onward and upward.

Angels are wonderful healers, but the archangels and the unicorns are *Master-healers*.

They, our unicorn friends, vibrate at an even higher energy level than the angels, and so their healing qualities are of the absolute maximum purity and strength just like the archangels and usually work at a very deep soul level. This is called Master-healing.

The angelic energies may bring you peace of mind, comfort, support, inspiration or just a comforting warm feeling.

The unicorn energies may bring you any of the above, but with an intensity that is off-the-scale!

The unicorns are blessed with not only these amazing healing powers, but because of their amazing heritage, also bring along the unique elements of magic and mystery.

It is these additions which make healing and communicating with the unicorns such a beautiful and wonderfully pure and magical experience.

There is a specially written healing meditation at the end of this chapter which brings in all the wonderful energies of the crystals, colours and the power and glory of the Angelic Kingdom, including the unicorns, of course.

There is a very special unicorn that you haven't met yet, called Star.

He is a more youthful unicorn than our old friend Omega! He is going to write some children's books on his own soon, but he wants to say a few words now. So here's Star!

'I've been waiting patiently in the wings for Adela to introduce me! At last...

Long ago, when days were long and bright, when I was so small you would never have even noticed me, I used to watch the ancient ones perform miracles of healing, and acts of deep compassion, and tenderness on all those who were in need.

There was no jealousy, no pride, no anger, no comparison or judgement.

We were all one.

No one was lonely, or bullied, or abused, or beaten, or neglected, or unloved.

Everyone was happy, in one big happy family.

I was so happy then.

I used to roll on my back, and kick my legs in the air.

The little ones, the children folk and the pixies and fairies played with me.

How we all laughed and sang.

How we played, and joked, danced and raced about.

The energies were pure and simple then.

Loving and Light.

Not a care in the world.

I don't remember any diseases, or arguments,

There wasn't any fighting,

There certainly wasn't any bloodshed.

I have come back now, older and wiser, but bringing with me those beautiful memories of days gone by.

I have come now to help bring back those days of Heaven on Earth.

I want to help all humanity, and bring healing and love to this tired, part-neglected and part-exploited planet of yours.

I am drawn particularly to the children folk, and want to bring joy and strength and courage into their lives if they are suffering in any way.

I want to encourage them to see the beauty in the world and in others.

After all, it is through the eyes of the children that the vision of the future is seen.

My wish is for all children to be loved, and to be well fed and have a roof over their head, and to be respected and valued.

My wish is for all children to have a voice that is HEARD in this land of noise and pollution.

My wish is for all children to know that they are all one people, whatever the colour of their skin, and that they are equal to others whether they are blind, deaf, disabled or different in any way.

I bring hope and happiness.

I bring peace of mind.

I bring joy and laughter.

I bring good health and healing.

I bring courage and clarity.

I bring the purest Love and

I bring the brightest Light.

I come to bridge the gap

Between Heaven and Earth.

I come with the company and blessings

Of my angel friends,

To lighten the lives

Of those that

Are weighed down with doubt and despair,

The agonies of abuse,

Torture and torment.

I bring my blessings

My Love is all encompassing,
All seeing, all enfolding, all embracing
And for the benefit of all.
I am Star.
I am from the Unicorn Kingdom,
May you open your arms up to me?
Like a baby to its mother,
And welcome me into your life
And feel my loving arms around you
Always and in all ways.
Bye for now!'

Thank you Star for your amazing, gently powerful healing and uplifting words.

Unicorns and angels can heal on many different levels.

We may be aware of their presence in dreams, meditations and visualizations.

The unicorns can bring love, peace of mind and deep relaxation. The angels are always a source of reassurance, protection and guidance.

We can also personally receive these wonderful energies directly through our own meditations, and simply asking them into our lives, and asking them to fill us with their loving Light.

Yes, YOU can!

We can experience the presence of unicorns in other ways. They are a powerful source of high energy, and can act as a catalyst in any challenging situation, or golden opportunity, in which you may find yourself.

You may have asked the unicorns for help in a certain

matter, and then you keep having an inner feeling that you should go to a certain place at a certain time.

The unicorns are magical indeed, and will do their utmost to ensure that you meet the people that you need to meet to help you on your spiritual journey.

Follow this inner voice, and see where the unicorns lead you!

(As long as it is safe and sensible to do so.)

Unicorns and angels can actually bridge the gap from imagination and the visualization of our dreams and meditations into reality, and actual practical aspects of our lives.

They bring us forward on our journey towards the light and enlightenment, to help and heal ourselves, our planet and all humankind.

Here is an inspirational message from the Angelic Kingdom,

All people
All humanity
All problems and confusions,
All can be touched and healed,
and brought nearer to God,
the Great White Spirit,
Father Sky and Mother Earth,
by the power and majesty
of these magnificent beings
The Unicorns
and their celestial friends
the Angels and Archangels

All children of the Universe
All together and all one
Singing, laughing and
supporting, guiding,
loving and embracing,
giving
STRENGTH where there is weakness,
POWER where there is abuse and control,
COURAGE where there is fear and pain,
PEACE where there is war and bloodshed,
LIGHT where there is darkness and despair,
PURITY where there is dirt and ugliness,
SUPPORT where there is failure and futility.

Let the STRENGTH and PURITY
of the angelic realm
uplift and empower you
to be strong and sure
in thought and word and deed.

Thank you.

The unicorns have the ability to bring us not only their healing powers, but because of their magical horn they can bring increased powers of intuition and psychic abilities to us.

The horn, which grows from the unicorn's third eye in the middle of their forehead, has an intensity of pure light which can gently open our own third eye, or brow **chakra**, to see beyond reality, and bring us more knowledge and closer to enlightenment and nearer to ascension.

What exactly are chakras?

We have a spiritual energy system within us and in our etheric body or aura which surrounds us. The energy system, within us, is made up of energy centres, which are called 'chakras'. This is the ancient language of Sanskrit's word for 'wheel'. The energy system around us is called the aura.

The seven major chakras or energy wheels are:
- the crown chakra, at the top of the head (violet)
- the brow or "third-eye" chakra, in the middle of the forehead (indigo)
- the throat chakra (blue)
- the heart chakra, in the centre of the chest (green)
- the solar plexus chakra, the area above the navel (yellow)
- the sacral chakra, below the navel (orange)
- the base or root chakra, at the base of the spine. (red)

A healthy chakra will be clear and balanced, and energy will be free-flowing into and out of each chakra.

When a chakra is in a state of balance, and clear, it will vibrate to the different colours of the rainbow, as indicated in the brackets. So, for example, the colour associated with the brow chakra is indigo.

These energy centres can become blocked and unbalanced and if the situation is not rectified disease can occur.

E.g. a blocked throat chakra, dealing with communication

and trust, could result in a sore throat or swollen glands.

A colour therapist/healer will probably use a **blue** colour, and a crystal healer will probably use a **blue** crystal, such as blue-lace agate or sodalite.

These are the colours for working on the throat chakra.

Complementary therapists, such as spiritual healers, Reiki practitioners etc. will work on the chakras, channelling energy, to promote healing and chakra balancing.

They will channel positive spiritual energies into each chakra to rebalance and energize or clear each chakra.

It is said that the chakras are the gateways to the soul.

Healing with unicorn energy is utilizing the same ancient energy healing which was first practised in Egypt about 5000 years ago.

The magic of unicorn energy is that it will find the source, however buried or hidden, of the spiritual disharmony, tension or conflict within you, and will heal at the deepest level of your soul.

The whole of the Angelic Kingdom are ready, and waiting to help you, just ASK and they will be at your side in a flash!

Let the magic continue…

Meditations of Magical Healing

Here are two healing meditations.

The first is specifically for the third-eye chakra, and the second is written to promote healing with colour. Both ask the Angelic Kingdom to help and support us.

It is important to note that these spiritual exercises are *complementary* to any traditional medical treatments that you may be receiving. They are not meant to be an alternative therapy or a substitute for medical advice and care, although they are totally compatible with them and highly beneficial practices.

One: A meditation to unblock and clear the brow or third-eye chakra.

As this chakra resonates to the specific colour of indigo, a deep royal blue, it is very helpful to have some blue-coloured crystals, to hold or to place nearby.

E.g. sodalite, lapis lazuli, azurite etc.

The three higher chakras, the throat, brow and crown, are connected to the areas of communication, self-expression, intuition, insights, psychic abilities, clairvoyance, our spiritual selves and the connection to our soul.

It would be quite suitable to have violet or purple crystals with you as well.

E.g. amethyst, flourite, sugilite etc.

Clear quartz is also fine for this exercise.

If you do not own any crystals, and are unsure which to purchase, then clear quartz is an excellent first buy.

It contains every colour within its structure, it is a master-healer, and it can be used for any situation or condition, whether it is an emotional, physical, mental or spiritual matter.

You really can't go wrong with quartz.

If you do not have many crystals, or if they are not of the above colours just try and 'see' if they feel right for you. Trust your intuition.

If in doubt, use the quartz!

After this exercise, hopefully your intuition will be heightened, and you will be more in tune with what seems right for you more often.

Before you commence this meditation try to find a time when you will not be disturbed, take the phone off the hook if it's safe to do so, choose a place in your house, garden or park (weather permitting!) where you feel safe and comfortable.

If at any stage you feel uncomfortable, anxious, or uneasy in any way gently open your eyes, take a few deep breaths and reassure yourself that everything is fine and all is as it should be.

If you wish to wear your clothes in the colours of blue, violet, or purple, then although not strictly necessary, this will also help the exercise.

Time to begin...**the first Meditation.**

Welcome friends to this special time and place.

This sacred space and a sacred time to embrace the pure and powerful energies of your magical and majestic friends of the Angelic Kingdom, especially the unicorns.

Supported as always and forever by your loyal and trusted guardian angel.

Now calling upon those fine celestial beings, the archangels, to enfold you and protect you in their strong and loving wings, now and always.

Start now to relax, and breathe deeply.

Knowing that you are totally protected and loved in this special place.

Focus on your breathing, nice and slowly and deeply.

Slowly and deeply.

Close your eyes, and know that you are safe and secure.

Surrounded and protected by your unicorn and angel friends.

Feel your body relax, your muscles warm and soft, your shoulders dropped and without tension, your legs and arms feeling heavy and soft.

Know that your feet are touching the ground/floor, and try to imagine that you have roots growing out of the soles of your feet, growing down into Mother Earth anchoring you firmly, safe and secure, grounded and still in touch with reality.

Now, your breathing is steady, and your body warm and relaxed, and your mind still, you are going to bathe yourself in a golden light.

Imagine yourself surrounded and enfolded in a beautiful golden light.

You may see a beautiful white unicorn surrounded in white clouds sending his strength and pure love to you.

Mentally call him to your side.

He stands by you and you are aware of his loving strength and support.

You connect with his powerful and pure energy and feel safe and secure.

You may feel the touch of an angel as they come closer to you.

You can now ask Archangel Michael to help you to release any negative thoughts you may be feeling.

Release them now.

Breathe them away.

Archangel Raphael will come to your side to support you in this healing moment if you ask him. He will come to your side, and wrap you in his comforting wings.

Breathing in, imagine the beautiful healing warm loving golden light coming down from your head over your shoulders, down your back, like a golden cloak, covering you with Love and Light.

Breathe this colour into your body, filling every pore and every cell with this healing warmth and loving light.

You are feeling relaxed and warm.

Full of a beautiful angelic light.

You are now ready to visualize a deep blue light, like the colour of a moonlit sky, a pure and intense indigo blue.

Feel the energies of your chosen crystals heighten this colour.

See this colour deeply in your mind's eye.

Now place the fingers of your dominant hand in the middle of your forehead, on the brow or third-eye and try and feel the deep blue colour in this spot.

Sense the colour.

Focused and strong,

Opening and clearing,

Balancing and cleansing,

Let the purity and strength of this magnificent colour illuminate your brow chakra and open your third eye.

Let this colour shine with clarity, and bring the wonderful gifts of intuition, and insights into your very soul.

Know that any fears or worries about your own psychic abilities will be dissolved, and know that as these gifts of inner vision and perception increase that you will always be mindful and use these gifts wisely, for the benefit of humanity and mankind.

Mentally ask the unicorn to help you to see more clearly through your third eye.

Ask the unicorn to help you to gently open your third eye.

Let the unicorn send out his loving light and powerful energies from his magical horn into your opening third-eye chakra.

Know that this is all happening as it should and as it is written in the Akashic records.

Be aware of any feelings which you may receive at this time.

Thank the universe, the unicorns and all the angelic hosts for their love and support in this meditation.

Gently, come back into waking consciousness, feel your feet, give them a little wiggle, have a stretch, slowly and gently open your eyes, and return to your surroundings.

As with any energy work it is a good idea to have a glass of water, wash your hands, and to ensure you are well grounded after this meditation.

Write any experiences in your journal as soon as possible, also any insights or feelings which may materialize.

Do not expect miracles immediately.

Give them a day or two!

Try not to be impatient, and just see if you begin to notice more psychic feelings.

Maybe time to treat yourself to a cup of tea.

Remember to always drink a glass or two of water after any meditation or spiritual exercise.

The second meditation is specifically written to focus on each chakra colour, and to aid in chakra balancing and healing. It is directed at the deep level of the soul, and is a beautiful way to connect with the Angelic Kingdom to bring you peace and tranquillity.

Two: A Meditation with Unicorns,
Ascended Masters, and Archangels.
Healing with colour and the Angelic Kingdom.

Welcome, my friend, to this special sacred place that you are going to create here, at this special sacred time in your life.

We ask that you be supported, and guided, as always, by the angelic realms and beyond.

Help you to stay grounded and protected as you embark on this loving journey of soul-healing towards deeper wisdom, and greater understanding, of yourself and others.

Start now to relax and breathe deeply.

Knowing that you are totally protected and loved in this special sacred space.

Focus on your breathing, nice and slowly and deeply.

Slowly and deeply.

Take a moment to call in your guardian angel, and any other helpers or guides you may have.

Trust and know that whether you can see them or not, that you have the love and support of your guardian angel, and the angelic realm of angels, archangels and unicorns.

Know that you are loved in this sacred healing space, and know that you are safe and secure, surrounded and protected by your chosen helpers.

Feel your body relax, your muscles warm and soft, your shoulders dropped and without tension, your legs and arms feeling heavy and soft.

Know that your feet are touching the floor, and that you are anchored and grounded to Mother Earth, now and always.

With each breath you feel calmer, more relaxed, more peaceful, and start to feel more loved than ever before.

Imagine now:

In each corner of your room is a beautiful golden unicorn radiating a pure and powerful golden-white light from their magnificent spiral horn into this sacred space around you, and you breathe in this beautiful light.

They bring you purity, peace, love and healing at a deep soul-level.

Their light is the most pure, undiluted, powerful, loving energy of deep healing.

It is gentle, warm and loving.

This is a sacred, healing space you have created here with your guardian angel, archangels and unicorns.

Know that this is a sacred and special time in your life.

Know that you are loved and supported by your guardian angel always.

These special unicorns will stay in their sacred, geometric positions, in each corner of the room, to the North, South, East and West, and generate their protective and powerful energies of love, healing and peace to you in this soul-healing meditation.

Breathe in the golden-white light.

Breathing in, imagine a beautiful healing, warm, loving golden-white light coming down from your head over your shoulders, down your back, like a golden cloak, covering you with Love and Light.

Breathe this colour into your body, filling every pore and every cell with this healing warmth, and loving light.

Open your heart.

Breathe in even more of this golden-white light, and now imagine it filling your heart, and heart chakra, touching your very soul.

Mentally, say the words your soul needs to hear:

I love, accept and approve of myself.

The Ascended Master, Saint-Germaine, comes to your sacred space today, bringing his wisdom and understanding.

He walked on the Earth plane, just as you are doing now, for many life times, and grew in his own spiritual abilities and psychic powers.

He wishes to bring you guidance, his ultimate protection, and courage.

He is connected to the high-frequency, violet-purple colour associated with the silver-violet flame.

He invites you to breathe in this violet-purple colour, and feel it flowing around your body, filling you with a deep sense of belonging and connection to the magic and mystery of the world about you.

The colour of violet resonates deeply with the crown chakra, at the top of your head.

Take a moment now to surround yourself with this spiritual, amethyst colour of violet-purple.

If you sense any deep-rooted fear, hurt or negative feelings try to visualize them being placed in the silver-violet flame of Saint-Germaine, and watch them dissolve and disappear.

Imagine now the colour of indigo, the colour of the night sky, and feel this colour seep sweetly and silently into your third-eye or brow chakra. Think of the majestic horn of the sacred unicorn coming out of their forehead, and remember your own intuition, and inner vision, and feel this indigo colour heighten your awareness and psychic perception.

I now ask Archangel Michael to join you at this special time.

He brings love and support from the Angelic Kingdom, and he brings you strength and courage.

His supreme power will help you at this time if

you need his help to combat any form of negative behaviour.

He will stand by you, a tower of strength, in your hour of need.

We welcome him to this sacred space, and we fill ourselves now with the intense blue and brilliant gold healing coloured light which he brings us.

Let us now breathe in these colours of blue and gold.

I now invite Archangel Raphael to join you in this sacred healing space.

He is the Archangel of Healing, and we welcome his warmth and unlimited supply of gentle, tender, loving healing energies at this time.

We envelop ourselves in the green and pink coloured light he brings us, to help heal our heart chakra.

Take a moment now to breathe in these special and sacred colours of Archangel Raphael, the beautiful greens and pinks, and imagine them filling your heart, and heart chakra, touching your very soul.

Place your hand on your heart for a moment, and sense the deep connection with your inner light, your holy centre, your inner spark, your SOUL, your Divine self, YOU.

That part of you which has been with you forever, and will live forever, and will never leave you, your SOUL.

Connect with that place, your sacred soul centre, and fill it with love and light.

Open your heart.

Take a few moments to relax in the peace and tranquillity of this sacred connection.

Know that you are loved, and know that you are accepted, and know that you are approved of in this sacred space.

I now invite Archangel Jophiel to join with you.

She brings you her golden yellow light of feminine angelic energy.

The 'Beauty of God'.

Let the intensity of her brilliant yellow light illuminate your soul.

She helps you to see the beauty in the world, and in your own lives.

Let us be inspired by her beauty, and awaken our souls to the wisdom and understanding which she can reveal to us.

Let us now breathe in the pure, sun yellow coloured light she brings us today, and always.

I now ask the ancient sun goddess Brigit to join you.

She is associated with fire, and brings the colours of flame reds and orange to warm and comfort you today.

Breathe in these Divine colours of red and orange.

Brigit is known as the triple goddess of the flame, and uses her flames to purify, increase fertility, creativity, and to promote deep intense healing.

Know that you are loved and protected by your friends and helpers of the Divine Kingdom.

Take some time now to allow the colours of the angelic realm, and ascended masters who are with you now, to cleanse, purify and heal you, and energize and clear your sensitive chakra system.

Relax, and do nothing, the warm waves of colour healing flow, and find their own way to those places where they need to be.

The golden-white light of the Angelic and Unicorn Kingdom.

The violet-purple of the Ascended Master, Saint-Germaine.

The indigo of the sacred Unicorn Kingdom,

The blues and gold of Archangel Michael.

The greens and pinks of Archangel Raphael.

The brilliant yellows of Archangel Jophiel.

The reds and orange from the ancient Brigit.

Know now, that these colours bring healing, at a deep level, to energize and enhance your delicate chakra energy system.

Know now that you can call upon these angels, archangels, unicorns and ascended masters at any time, whenever you need their love and support.

Know now, that you are a pure being of Love and Light; your Divine spark is shining and bright,

You are a pure being, accept and love yourself,

You are a beautiful soul in a beautiful body,

You are a pure being and can shine brightly to help bring

Love and Light to the planet.

You make a difference

You are special and unique

Know now that you are loved and safe and supported always.

Now you can thank your guardian angel, all your guides, supporters, angels, archangels, unicorns and ascended masters.

Take a moment now to mentally thank them in your own way, and allow the healing energy and light to settle and take root in your mind, body and soul.

Start now to come back into the room, back to waking consciousness, wriggle your fingers and toes, gently and slowly open your eyes...

The meditation is now complete.

Take a few moments to gently return to waking consciousness.

Time for a glass of water.

Maybe a cup of tea would be appreciated.

If you feel slightly light-headed, you can stamp your feet, have a breath of fresh air, and wash your hands.

All these actions will ground you again.

Meditation is perfectly safe, and extremely therapeutic.

I hope that you have had some positive experiences during this chapter, and that you have lots to write in your journal!

CHAPTER FOUR

Unicorns, Energy thieves and protection

In the last chapter we began to think about our own spiritual energy, and our chakras or energy wheels.

The level of spiritual energy that we can achieve, and the state of our chakras helps to determine how we function (w)holistically, that is in mind, body and soul, as a complete or whole person.

Our chakras are like little power stations, sending out and receiving energy 24/7.

This energy has many names; it can be called, by those who believe in God, the Divine power. Some people may prefer to call it the Universal Life Force, or the source of never-ending unconditional love.

In Chinese cultures it is called Ki, or Chi, as in Reiki, and Tai Chi. The ancient language of Sanskrit names it prana, or the life breath.

Whatever we choose to call it, it is both precious and priceless, and when we've got it we really need to hang on to it.

This is where energy thieves come in!

What exactly are energy thieves?

When we are working positively, in thought, and word and deed, and we are trying to live a life without fear and confusion, and surrounding ourselves with a warm and loving light then our chakras will be operating at their highest potential at that time.

This manifests itself as a life of harmony, and in perfect balance.

It is of the utmost importance, for our own well-being, to try to live our lives in such a way, through diet, exercise, healing, meditation etc., to keep this optimum balance.

This doesn't happen overnight, and can take several lifetimes!

However, as soon as our intention is set on this spiritual practice then positive results begin to happen.

Every time we engage with our spiritual self our soul smiles, heals a little more, and magically our energy rises to a higher level. Our chakras begin to spin more smoothly, and spiritually we are in good shape.

When we achieve harmony and balance in our lives we can radiate health and vitality.

The more bright and clear the chakras become, particularly the heart chakra, the more we seem to radiate Love and Light, and almost glow with a charismatic presence.

This is wonderful to experience, a marvellous example for others to emanate, but, unfortunately, also a tempting source of pure energy for someone feeling run-down and flat themselves.

This is where PROTECTION comes in.

Watch out, there are energy thieves about!

So what exactly are these energy thieves?

How often have you felt really positive, radiant, vibrant and happy and gone out, begun to talk to someone, and begun to feel all your energy draining away?

On the other hand you may have been feeling listless, depressed, and rather negative, and then you've met an old friend who was so amazingly uplifting, positive and cheerful that you began to feel totally energised!

This is how, at a subconscious level, an energy exchange can occur.

We can lose some of our beautiful, positive energy if we let someone literally drain it away from us. Maybe, they could upset us with an insensitive comment, which affects us at a deep level. They may start a very negative or angry conversation with us which wounds us, and makes us feel down or deflated.

Protection is called for!

This is how high-energy people, like YOU, can ensure that your precious life force is not tapped into, and sucked away by energy drainers.

On the other hand, Lightworkers may have achieved clear and balanced chakras, through time and the hard work of purification, therapy, meditation, prayer etc. They may decide to share the benefit of this high-energy state which they have achieved to help to channel positive, spiritual energies of Love and Light to others,

E.g.through a session of spiritual healing, Reiki etc.

This is totally different scenario to having your energies removed without realising it.

The miracle of channelling energy is that it does not

deplete your own energy supply, as you are purely the channel for the spiritual energy and unconditional love to pass along.

However, if someone is a magnetic healer then this is when they use their *own* energies, and this is likely to drain and de-energise them completely.

Happily, there are numerous methods that we can use to protect our personal energies.

How exactly can we protect our own spiritual energy? What exactly is spiritual protection?

Remember that all the following methods of energy protection can be strengthened, and enhanced by asking for help from your unicorn friends and the angelic realms.

However, later I am going to describe some specific protection procedures which involve the Unicorn Kingdom, and are highly effective, high-level and simple to use.

Meanwhile, there are many forms of aura and energy protection, and it is sometimes a question of trial and error to find the method that seems to be the most effective for you.

It is a personal choice, and you may well develop your own strategy for any negative situations.

The angels and unicorns will be delighted to help, and certainly if you really want the heavy gang in the picture then Archangel Michael is your man, or should I say angel!

Always remembering, that if the situation is very dark and challenging that he also has the band of Warrior Angels to bring with him.

Protection for the Protector.

Just ask him along.

The first, most easy method of energy protection is to totally encase and surround yourself, mentally, in a

' Protection Bubble'.

This protects your chakras and your auras to prevent any leakage by energy thieves, or if you find yourself in a hostile or unfriendly environment.

Simply *visualise* yourself enclosed in a beautiful bubble, which goes over your head and under your feet in an egg-shaped sphere.

This bubble can be filled with light. The colour of the light you choose is intuitively which seems appropriate for you at the time. The bubble is best imagined to be about 12 to 18 inches around your body.

E.g. the colour pink would be a gentle and healing light, particularly appropriate in a difficult relationship situation.

Gold would be a very highly spiritual colour, if you were in a situation surrounded by non-believers or sceptics.

Silver would be a very clear and sharp colour, if you were in a situation where your truth and integrity may be questioned, or if you needed to be incisive and quick-witted.

Trust yourself and your intuition to choose the colour and size of bubble that you need at this particular time.

This bubble will allow your own positive vibrations to move out of the sphere, and let other positive energies permeate through into your space, but your intention of strength and protection will prevent any negative energy from entering your protective bubble.

You are in control of this bubble, and so if you want to remove it, just envisage it disappearing in a flash. Otherwise, you can keep it in place as long as you feel that you need to.

Your energies will remain intact, and safe.

It may sound rather strange, but it is effective, and really works!

It is a 'golden oldie' in terms of protection, but is still an effective method. Someone did say to me that they thought it was like putting on an old faded tee-shirt!

An add-on to this protection is the **Solar plexus 'metallic' disc** visualization.

If you are going to be in a very demanding, negative and emotionally disturbing situation you can use the protective bubble, and reinforce the protection by a further heavy-duty visualization, as follows.

(Is it really totally necessary to put yourself in this position anyway? Is there an easier alternative?)

Our solar plexus chakra, situated in the area above your tummy button, is the spiritual 'entry point' for the major emotional feelings of fear, sadness, anxiety, anger, distress and guilt.

If we feel threatened by someone's anger or rage it will possibly feel like an actual kick in the stomach.

Sometimes, we actually protect this chakra subconsciously. We may put a cushion over our stomach whilst we are arguing, or hold our coat or handbag in front of us if we feel threatened in any way.

The more sensitive we are, the more likely we are to be adversely affected by negative energies, and so the more important it is for us to protect ourselves.

If a negative situation or encounter occurs, out of the blue, where we are subjected to an 'attack' of this nature we can swiftly, mentally slide the 'metallic' disc over our stomach or solar plexus area.

(Obviously, move away, out of the firing-line, if we can.)

You can visualize the disc in bronze, gold, silver, pewter or copper, whichever seems to suit your purpose and the situation in the best way.

This gives immediate protection, and prevents letting further negative energies into your chakra system.

Some healers use an alternative to a 'metallic' disc, and visualize a disc of light instead.

The procedure is the same, for both types of disc, and all are equally effective.

Most Lightworkers, healers and other therapists who are working with vulnerable, ill or depressed people will usually automatically put on a protective layer just in case.

In fact, many professional and business people could benefit from using this procedure, as they can be subjected to negativity by nature of their job, and the emotional state of their customers and/or patients:

E.g. bank managers, doctors, nurses, etc.

Different therapists will develop their own individual methods of spiritual protection, and use whichever is most effective for them.

Some other systems used are: To imagine the blue cloak of Archangel Michael wrapped around your whole head and body, or to mentally breathe in the Light and Love of Jesus Christ.

There is a spiritual protection exercise called The Christ Light at the end of this chapter.

For some, the power of the Divine is all the spiritual support that they feel they need.

We are all special, and unique, and as in all things spiritual we should seek the right method for ourselves. As long as we remember to use something, then that's fine!

As well as these visualizations many people take comfort in the use of **crystals** as a protective measure.

There are many books written on the subject of individual crystals, and their varied uses for healing, protection and of course their decorative values!

However, the most common crystal used to absorb negative energies is probably smoky quartz. This is readily available, and reasonably priced.

Crystal healers will use different stones and crystals for each individual person and circumstance, using their experience and intuition.

E.g. Black tourmaline can absorb negativity, and amber or jet will protect your own energies.

Turquoise is also a powerfully protective stone, used for generations by the Native American Indians.

Some people will suggest that thinking about needing protection is a negative way of thinking, and that it is a self-fulfilling prophesy.

In other words if you think negative thoughts expect negative actions.

However, I would respond that if you were a builder working on a building site it would be sensible (and legal) to wear your yellow helmet, and steel capped boots, just in case you're hit by a wayward flying brick!

Be prepared!

If at any time, during a meditation or spiritual exercise, you feel uneasy or anxious in any way, maybe this is not the best time for you to be doing this work, so calmly and confidently surround yourself with a powerful white loving light.

Then direct a beam of the most pure, bright, white light out of your heart chakra in front of you, thinking and visualizing LOVE.

Open your eyes, take a deep breath and have a glass of water or a cup of tea!

You can always return to the exercise at another time.

If you are unsure in a meditation if the angel or person that has appeared to you is who they say they are, then you can ask those 3 times, and under Universal Law they must reveal their true identity.

I.e. are you my guardian angel?

Are you my guardian angel?

Are you my guardian angel?

Hopefully, they will affirm their identity.

If not, then focus your intention, and direct a beautiful beam of Love and Light in their direction, and they will immediately vanish.

The angels, archangels and unicorns are all heavenly

beings and will help in any way they can, whether it be for protection, comfort, guidance, inspiration, or support in any way.

The angels usually need to be ASKED, and then as long as the request is loving, genuine and for the best reasons they will be delighted to help.

If you are ever tempted to send out a negative energy to another person I advise you to think again.

Not only will this be noted on your karmic record, but the negative force will be rebounded onto you tenfold!

The old saying

'What goes around comes around'… comes to mind.

Be aware!

Beware!

You may feel that *you* are the subject of 'psychic attack'. This is very rare, and most unlikely. However, it is my belief that we are only ever sent anything that we are capable of dealing with ourselves. You can use all the methods that I have described previously, but in addition you can use the **'Mirror shield'.**

I.e. imagine that you are placed in the middle of a screen/shield of a circle of mirrors. The reflective side is pointing outwards.

You can send out a continual beam of the most powerful LIGHT, and strongest LOVE from your safe haven behind the mirrors.

This ensures that you are in a positive position surrounded by Love and Light, and any (if any!) negative energy is sent in your direction, the mirrors will deflect it back to the sender.

It is a perfectly safe and peaceful method to use for your own peace of mind. In a spiritual sense it also gives the sender a piece of your mind!

Of course, the Angelic Kingdom of angels, archangels and unicorns are an amazing source of powerful protection in the spiritual sense. If we imagine them by our side, and **ask** for their LOVE and LIGHT they will wrap their wonderful wings around us, and keep us safe and secure always.

Here are two specialised unicorn protection methods to keep us safe and secure.

If we feel threatened or endangered, spiritually, then we can immediately visualise a circle of unicorns, a **Circle of Light**, surrounding us, with their radiant horns pointing into the centre of the circle (over our head) with their beams of golden-white light converging above us.

They may all be white unicorns, some or all black ones, pink, purple, rainbow, striped or polka-dotted!

Whichever you feel is the colour that you need to protect you, then that is fine.

If during a meditation, healing, or other spiritual work you see someone struggling with negativity, or it may even be yourself, then the unicorns have another set of tools in their box of protection.

You can use any of the methods that I've detailed earlier, but you may feel the need to utilise the following technique.

Visualise the challenging situation, mentally remove yourself or the other person from it, and then let the unicorns surround and enclose the darkness in a **Cocoon**

of Light, and then imagine that they are stamping their hooves onto this negative energy until it totally disappears.

Keep breathing love and light onto the situation.

Know that you are safe and secure.

Breathe deeply and relax.

These are the powerful energies of the Angelic Kingdom of unicorns at work.

If unicorn energy is involved EXPECT THE UNEXPECTED.

Whatever works for us, however unlikely or unusual, let's also ACCEPT THE UNEXPECTED.

Last but not least, we should not forget to include the protection of our spirit power animal.

Power animals not only protect, inspire and teach us, but also can heal and help us to develop and move on spiritually as well.

What exactly is a power animal?

A power animal is an 'animal' which brings us the power of that particular species, in spiritual form, not the furry or feathered kind!

They are spirit guides in animal form.

They can be a wonderful part of our support group on our spiritual journey, and are every bit as powerful and protective as the Angelic Kingdom.

The power animals feel most at home, and can be found with the elementals, the pixies, fairies, elves etc. in the gardens, jungles, forests, skies and oceans of the spiritual world.

They are very happy to be contacted, and happy to help us mere humans in our spiritual endeavours.

Each of us has an individual opinion, and judgment of every animal. Our life experiences obviously influence how we think about certain animal.

We may not consider a dog to be 'Man's Best Friend' if we were bitten by the neighbour's canine when we were a child.

When we learn more about power animals, and how to discover our own animal helper, healer or guide, remember that it is **always** what that animal represents to **you**, and how you perceive the qualities and traits of the species **yourself**, whatever a book may say.

You are on your own spiritual journey, and you have many helpers and guides to support, protect, heal, teach and inspire you.

Power animals are a part of this group, if you want them to be.

There are absolutely no rules for what can be a power animal, and what cannot.

We meet our friends, the power animals, in our dreams and meditations. They can introduce themselves to us in real life, or through television programmes, magazine articles and photographs, and many other wonderful and unusual ways!

Omega, the most sacred of the winged unicorns, says:

'My word, what a very fascinating subject, you've embarked upon here.

Expect the unexpected!

Very often, it appears to me, that the unusual or unplanned aspect of your life is where you seem to learn the greatest lessons.

The people, the places or indeed the animals who come unexpectedly into your life can be a wonderful new source of healing, or learning.

Once you have been introduced to your power animal friend I am sure that your life will take on new meaning, new direction and new understanding.

Embrace your power animal.

Trust him (or her!).

Know that he has come into your life at this particular time for a very special reason.

Look for his strengths, and his fine qualities, and bring them into your own life.

Let him help and support you.

Let him love and protect you.

Let him reassure and encourage you.

Let him console and comfort you.

Let him give you strength and confidence.

Let him nurture and heal you.

Let him (or her!) walk beside you on this special journey, on this beautiful path to joy and peace and enlightenment.

He may not be the animal that you expected, but do not be in any doubt that he will be the animal that you NEED at this particular time.

Accept him into your life.

It will be all the greater and more fulfilling with him at your side.'

Thank you Omega.

Could a unicorn be a power animal?

A unicorn would be a magnificent, majestic and magical power animal.

There is every good reason to accept the unicorn as a most magnificent blessing if he (or she!) comes to you as your power animal.

They symbolize all the qualities that a horse would bring you as a power animal; that is, freedom, independence, strength, friendliness, power and mobility, coupled with all the angelic qualities of love, compassion, peace and purity.

Add to this mix the unicorn's wonderfully special qualities of innocence, magic, protection, purity, master-healing and majestic power.

Certainly, the unicorn is an amazing Divine mixture of celestial energy and power, and this is certainly a very special and unique power animal.

Available to anyone, just ask him to come to your side, and wait.

If you are lucky enough to have more than one unicorn, as a friend or power animal, it is indeed a blessing.

A blessing of unicorns.

The following is a short list of the most popular power animals, and a short description of their qualities. There are several books available which can give more detailed information on each of the animals. The shamans, and the Native American peoples, and other indigenous tribes have very similar sacred animals and birds.

However, it is what the animal means to YOU which is of paramount importance.

Here are some popular power animals, and their general meanings.

Bear – revered for their wisdom.
Beaver – spirit of hard work, and persistence.
Deer – harmony.
Eagle – vision, courage, freedom, wisdom.
Hawk – focus, pride.
Horse – freedom, mobility, power, friendship.
Lion – courage, nobility.
Owl – wisdom, new beginnings.
Peacock – dignity, pride, royalty.
Raven – magic, healing between light and dark.
Rabbit – fertility, creativity.
Snake – rebirth, healing, transmutation/change.
Swan – grace, love, purity.
Wolf – guardian, family, storytelling.

The power animal may be with you for a short time, he may come and go, and some may stay with you forever.

They may even be cartoon animals, prehistoric or extinct. There are not any hard and fast rules here. One of my most supportive and powerful power animals is a beautiful, enormous woolly mammoth. She is very happy for me to share that with you. Sometimes power animals are rather reserved and private.

It is an absolute joy to name your power animal, just as you would name any member of your family. A name may come to you immediately, or you may feel that the animal has given you his name in a dream or meditation.

Do not question it. Believe it. However strange it may be. Go with it.

In one of my workshops recently, during the meditation, someone had a very unusual looking unicorn appear to her who she said closely resembled a donkey and who wanted to be called Neddy! He had winked at her and given her a wonderful smile.

She was feeling rather low beforehand, and after this magical encounter was grinning from ear to ear. Accept what comes. Expect the Unexpected, and Accept the Unexpected!

All power animals can be a source of infinite joy and reassurance, and bring love and empowerment into your life.

They can also bring humour, healing and harmony.

Most definitely though they bring PROTECTION.

Many people associate them exclusively with shamanism, which is understandable as they are part and parcel of that culture.

However, power animals are very happy to walk beside anyone, whatever their age, sex, race, faith or culture!

ENJOY THEIR COMPANY,

THEY ENJOY YOURS!

You have all the means at your fingertips to feel safe and secure in your spiritual pursuits…

ENJOY!

Let the magic continue…

A fun way to look out for your power animal

The ancient Celtic Druid seers had some wonderful ways to commune with nature to look for signs, omens and to try to predict future events.

I.e. divination.

One of the methods they used over 2000 years ago, starting during the first century BC, was the art of nephomancy, which we are going to use to try and find our power animal.

What on earth is it?

Nephomancy is the ancient practise of cloud divination.

So we are going to look into the skies, and see if we can recognise animal or bird shapes in the cloud formations.

Mad?

Absolutely not!

On a personal note here, whilst I was attending a therapist's retreat I had picked the giraffe from my power animal oracle cards for guidance for the rest of the day. I had told the group, and whilst eating my breakfast I looked out of the window.

There for all to see was the instantly recognisable, enormous giraffe-shaped cloud.

The only problem was that no-one had a camera handy.

It would have been almost impossible to have had such an amazing verification any other way than by this method of nephomancy, as there are not many giraffes in Wales!

Some of the more unusual methods of divination, which *may* seem a little strange, are:

cromniomancy – divination by onion sprouts.
margaritomancy – divination by bouncing pearls.
myomancy – divination by rodent behavior.
geloscopy – divination by laughter.

However, I'm not suggesting any of these methods to find your power animal.

This makes the art of nephomancy seem quite a normal pursuit.

The best time to do this is when the clouds are of the cumulus variety. I.e. white and fluffy.

For the first time choose a warm, fine day with a bright and still sky with plenty of clouds to observe. This will make it much easier for you.

Relax, and find a quiet spot where you will be undisturbed.

Ask the Angelic Kingdom to help you to recognise

the animal or bird which you need for support at this particular time.

It is entirely possible that you may, in fact, see a unicorn or angel shape in the clouds.

Don't make my mistake, try and remember your camera.

Look to the skies with your questions, and let the universe show you the answer in the clouds!

Write your experiences in your journal, with photographic evidence if you have it.

EXERCISE FOUR (B)

'The Christ Light'

A powerful and protective energy.

How can I connect with this energy?

Christ energies are magnifying, and growing ever stronger, today…Now.

Healers, who have never worked with Jesus Christ before, are now being introduced to Him.

His energies are very important for today, and especially since the Winter Solstice of 2012.

That time of the great shift of spiritual energy and the great opportunity for spiritual advancement.

The healing powers of Jesus, miraculous in any religion or belief system, are coming back, and helping therapists, counsellors, teachers, healers and all Lightworkers in their work.

He will help you personally, and His energies will help to lift the world towards the New Golden Age of Love and Light that the dawn of 2012 has heralded in for all mankind.

One night I was thinking about how to refresh and revive my own methods of protecting myself spiritually. I meet lots of different people, in all sorts of circumstances, and so need to protect my own energies.

Then I had a dream where I was sitting on the sand, and as I brushed the sand away, there was a book called 'The Christ Light', and as I brushed the sand off that book, there was another, and another, all called 'The Christ Light'.

The following morning I was contemplating my dream. I realized that the book title was just the beginning of a beautiful method, which was then channelled to me, about how to breathe in the Light of Christ for protection from the inside out!

I would like to share 'The Christ Light' with you, and hope you enjoy using it for protection, but it can be used equally well for self-healing or relaxation.

'THE CHRIST LIGHT'.

You can create a sacred space by your own intention, or by saying a few words, such as these:

'I am setting aside this special and sacred time to create a sacred space for me to connect with, and breathe in The Christ Light, for my highest good, and for the benefit of myself and others'.

Relax, and breathe nice and slowly and deeply.

Know that you are safe and secure.

Know that you are surrounded, and protected by the Angelic Kingdom of unicorns, angels and archangels.

Now imagine, as you breathe in, that The Christ

Light comes into your heart chakra, and fills you with a golden-white light.

You feel this light spread around your body, every pore, every cell, every bone, every muscle, every tissue, every part of your body is filled with this magnificent feeling of a warm, loving, healing, protective beautiful light.

It has a purity, and gentle power, and intensity that you have never experienced before.

The Christ Light is pure LOVE, and pure LIGHT, and brings you total PEACE and total PROTECTION whenever you need it.

You can start each day by breathing in The Christ Light, and top it up throughout the day if you need to.

I think that it is both a beautiful and simple spiritual exercise, and I hope that you enjoy using it as much as I do.

It also is very **powerful**, and it works.

CHAPTER FIVE

Purification or 'Lightening up'!

In the last chapters we have gained some powerful spiritual friends to accompany us on our journey, not least the unicorns.

We have gained more knowledge about our spiritual energy, and how to protect it.

We can now move forward onto the next stage of our spiritual development, and focus on our **purification**, or in more down-to-Earth language the 'clean-up' or 'ditching the dark stuff'!

What exactly is purification?

According to the dictionary it is 'to become pure, to cleanse from foreign or hurtful matter, to free from guilt, from ritual uncleanness, or barbarisms in language'.

This promises to be an interesting chapter.

I'm sure that if we need to free our language from barbarisms, and cleanse our ritual uncleanness it will be a great relief to all our friends and family that we are going to embark on this purification process!

In more spiritual terms, it could be described as becoming more pure, by removing negativity and negative energy from ourselves and our environment, or both.

Purification is actually a large part of our spiritual journey taking us towards enlightenment. We 'lighten-up' as we cleanse, and as we remove this dark and heavy negativity we become lighter in all ways, and more pure. This in turn raises our spiritual energy to a higher level.

It is bringing us one step nearer to the illumination of our very being or soul.

The Angelic Kingdom is delighted to help us out with this. In particular, Archangel Gabriel is the one in charge of the purification process.

Coupled with the company of the unicorns, whose exact job specification has helping out human souls move towards PEACE and PURITY at the top of their list, we can't go far wrong.

Before we start to become overwhelmed or dispirited at this point, here are a few wise words from our friend Omega, who always seems to pop up at the times when we need him most:

'My friends, if you could see the impact of negative thoughts, words and deeds on your energies, and your auras, you would be horrified.

Oh, my goodness gracious me!

Dark thoughts of anger, deceit, jealousy, hatred and fear put dark, heavy colours around you.

Every step you take will be an uphill struggle, like wading through thick sludgy treacle, sticky and uncomfortable.

Please, please try to think positive thoughts of love, peace, purity, joy and beauty.

You will shine, and radiate clear, bright, vibrant colours in your aura.

You will draw others to you, wanting to share and join you in your warm and positive energy.

You will feel lighter, and more connected to your higher consciousness, your soul.

Angel and unicorn messages will start to come through in wonderful and surprising ways.

We want you to be successful in your journey to connect with us, and so we will help.

Please call on us for our support and encouragement.

Call on myself, Omega, and my friends when you are trying to lead a life pure in thought and word and deed.

We are all very delighted to help you in your fine endeavours, and will help you every step of the way, on this your journey of purification and LOVE.'

Thank you Omega, that's very encouraging, so let's get started…

What is the first step towards personal purification?

Sorry to be so very personal, but the first question has to be:

Are we clean?

This is not just about personal hygiene, and getting the deodorants and shampoos spraying and foaming, but trying to keep our thoughts and feelings clean as well.

This is not to say that you'll never have a good laugh at a dirty joke, or smutty innuendo, but where will we draw the line?

Is it acceptable to laugh at a joke in which the punch line is racist?

Will we buy a cheap mobile phone which we really know has been stolen?

You have been given £5 too much change, will you give it back to the shop assistant?

The restaurant bill has not included the wine in the total. Do we tell them?

Sometimes, we seem to have a little voice (or even a loudhailer!) in our ear which encourages us to fail in our endeavours to live a life which is more pure.

Sometimes, it is rather difficult to be completely honest.

Sometimes, we try to protect other people's feelings by being less than honest, or 'being economical with the truth' as a politician may say, or we may try to justify our behaviour when we really know the truth of the matter.

At these times of challenge, we can call on Omega and his unicorn friends in the Angelic Kingdom to help us to do the right thing!

The unicorns and angels will be delighted to help us out with our dilemmas.

After all, the unicorns are the most powerful symbol of purity, so this is right up their street!

Helping humans on their purification process is the top of their Divine Job Specification.

So we should make it our business to make our first priority, our first job to enlist the help and support of the Unicorn Kingdom; it's their business, after all.

Let's harness their power to help us on our journey towards illumination and enlightenment, or in other words 'lightening-up'!

What else can help us to purify ourselves?

On a very practical level, what we eat and drink affects our purity.

The body is the temple of the soul, and we should try to worship it! Perhaps we should not feed it junk, processed or fatty foods if we can avoid it. I have read that although in theory the human heart has the capability to survive for 400 years, man can destroy it in 40.

Food for thought.

What can we do to purify ourselves spiritually?

The greatest purifier of all is LOVE.

Running a very close second place is the powerful purification force of LIGHT.

Love and Light are the most powerful purifiers of all.

The most powerful symbol of purity has to be the UNICORN.

So the **first** thing we need to do in the purification process is enlist the help and support of the Unicorn Kingdom.

Ask them to help you, and ask the Angelic Kingdom to come on board as well.

Remember that the archangel specifically in charge of purification is Archangel Gabriel, who will be delighted to help.

Surrounded by so much loving energy you cannot fail to be swept along on your path towards enlightenment.

Let's press onward on this spiritual journey. The steps towards self-purification are;

- Purifying your thoughts…easier said than done… trying to *catch* your negative…or rather 'non-positive' thoughts of anger, fear, guilt, lust, jealousy, hate etc. and then trying to change them into a positive. If you can catch them, write them down immediately, and then shred them or ceremoniously burn them! We have approximately 60,000 thoughts a day and so we're bound to have some that are less than perfect.

- Releasing negative thoughts, behaviour patterns etc. We could at this point ask for specific help from Archangel Zadkiel, who is the Archangel in charge of Transmutation. Transmutation is the process of changing negatives into positives.

The exercise, Brigit's Fire Wheel, at the end of this chapter will help us to deal with negative thoughts.

Another step towards self-purification is

- To acknowledge the shadow side of our soul. However much we try to be light, we are only human, and have a darker side as well. If we look within, and are honest with ourselves, we find areas of repressed anger, fear, shame, guilt, loss and lots of other wonderful qualities!

If we work on these findings, bring our deeply buried emotions up to the surface, face up to our dark side, and acknowledge the shadow then we can move forward spiritually at a great pace. Sometimes we have to accept that our soul may have scars, called samskaras, that are too deep to be healed, and will be part of our psyche forever. This does not harm or hinder our soul-journey, or stop us becoming lighter. In fact it can help us in our Lightworking, as we can use these painful soul memories to empathise with and heal others. This in turn will release much healing energy into the universe. This darkness helps others to the Light.

As the famous psychotherapist Carl Jung said:

'One does not become enlightened by imagining figures of Light, but by making the darkness conscious.'

The unicorns will help us in these endeavours.

They will take us to the places we need to go.

They will lead us to the people we need to meet.

They will stand by us as we work through our pain

To find the wisdom hidden beneath.

They will remind us of the saying:

'Without the darkness we can't see the stars.'

On this difficult part of our journey we need all the love and support we can find.

The ascended masters, those great spiritual healers and teachers who help us with our other spiritual friends, have lived lives on earth as human beings.

Unlike the angels and archangels who have always been angels and archangels, the ascended masters actually know how very difficult life on earth can be.

They have walked the earth planes, and they know about human nature and they know the pull of the dark side.

They are here to help, guide, encourage, support, lead, inspire and heal with their wisdom and love.

The energies of the great masters: Jesus Christ, St. Francis of Assisi, and particularly John the Baptist are very strong at the present time.

Very powerful, protective, pro-active and very PRESENT.

These steps towards self-purification, illumination, enlightenment and spiritual attainment bring us nearer to the ultimate ascension of our soul.

So, if you decide to be more spiritual, and try and live a more peaceful, harmonious and loving life then you will be drawn to people, places and pursuits that encourage these endeavours.

Interestingly, you may find that your choice of friends and companions may start to change.

If friends make you feel uneasy, strained, anxious, angry or depressed it may be time to reduce the time you spend with them.

These negative qualities will impact on your own sense of well-being, and actually drain your own energies.

There is no need for any confrontation or bad feeling with these people. It is likely that there will just be a gentle drift apart without any ill-effects.

As you become more aware, and actually try to raise your own spiritual energy level, the Universe will respond almost immediately and send more like-minded individuals into your surroundings.

The next chapter will describe how we can purify our environment, and create our own sacred space. If we try to purify ourselves, and transmute negative energies into positive ones then we start to raise our own personal energy level to a higher spiritual frequency.

This in turn raises the energy of the planet, and brings us nearer to the days of Heaven on Earth, which is the very reason that the unicorns have returned to help us!

The following spiritual exercise is a high level, high energy and high frequency method of self-purification which I hope you will enjoy doing.

It is called Brigit's Fire Wheel, but there is no need to worry about calling the fire brigade, it's all very safe!

Let's get purifying…

EXERCISE FIVE

Brigit's Fire Wheel

This exercise was channelled to me by the ancient warrior goddess Brigit. It is specifically aimed at healing at the soul level, and is a powerful method of self-purification.

Brigit certainly has the intensity and power to purify our souls at the deepest level.

She is a sun goddess, and is associated with fire.

So if you begin to feel very hot, and start to perspire during the exercise this is a sure sign that she is indeed working alongside you!

She is the female equivalent of Archangel Michael, and will bring you warmth, courage, and an intense balance of feminine and masculine energy and power.

The exercise combines the power of the circle, a sacred shape symbolising eternity, perfection, safety, oneness or completion and power, with the many purification qualities of the element of FIRE, together with the presence of the ancient sun goddess Brigit.

As Brigit channelled this exercise especially for us she will support each and every one of us throughout this process of purification.

Time to start,

Relax, breathe nice and slowly and deeply,

Begin to visualise her fire-wheel of the purifying flame,

With this fire there is no contamination, as the flames purify, your fears are burnt away for good!

Imagine now the power of the circle, rotating slowly and surely, like a wheel suspended from the ceiling, just like an old-fashioned light fitting turning gently and safely and burning brightly with the purifying flames of the goddess Brigit.

Keep this visualisation in your mind, relax, and concentrate on your breathing...

Nice and slowly and deeply.

Ground yourself by imagining roots growing from the soles of your feet anchoring you down into Mother Earth, safe and secure.

Ask that Brigit joins you now, supporting and guiding you through this spiritual exercise.

Let her words speak to you, and find a place in your heart and soul.

Brigit says,

'I will help and heal,

I will burn through the barriers of darkness and fear,

I will purify and cleanse your beautiful wounded soul,

You are a Lightworker, and need to burn brightly with

The Love of God, and the Light of the world,
Fear not,
Be not afraid,
This is happening now, as it should,
As it was laid down, directed,
And so written,
Now is the time to throw caution to the wind,
Release your fears, doubts and confusions,
Open your heart to the love and warmth of
The Divine.
I am Brigit, and I have been with you,
For light years,
Past, present and future,
Clear the way,
Light the Light within you,
Glow with the warmth of the love
Which only God can fire,
Deep within your very soul,
Love and compassion,
Tenderness and purity,
Knowledge and wisdom,
Beauty and peace,
Friendship,
Sisterhood and brotherhood,
True Love,
Empathy and sincerity,
Serenity and silence,
The gifts of the heart,
The qualities of a Perfected soul,

> *Open your heart to the love of God,*
> *Release all your fears*
> *Into the purifying flame*
> *Of the fire-wheel,*
> *And fill your heart and soul*
> *With a perfect love that*
> *Surpasses all understanding,*
> *Now and always,*
> *Harmony and Healing are yours.'*

These are the words of Brigit.

Now I ask that the Angels of Purification supervise, protect and guide you at this sacred time of soul-healing and purification.

Take some time now,

To ask that any old vows that you may have made in this life or past lives, which are not of any use or purpose any more, may be rescinded and released to the flames,

Do that now! Imagine you are mentally throwing these vows onto the fire-wheel.

To ask that any karmic debris, which is draining your energy and has now served its purpose, may be acknowledged and thanked for the life-lessons you have learnt from it, but can now be released to the flames.

Do that now!

To ask that any 'cords' which are connecting you to any

relationships, known or unknown to you, either in this life or others, which are not now serving your highest good and are draining your life force, can now be cut and released to the flames.

Do that now!

To ask that any limiting beliefs, issues, worries, fears, negative feelings, doubts and confusions can now be disentangled safely from your heart centre and soul, the learning safe and secure, but the worn-out and old thoughts which no longer serve you well and are restricting your spiritual growth, can now be released to the flames.

Do that now!

Know that now that you are healed and purified at a deep soul level.

Know that your heart and soul are now completely filled with love.

Know that you are loved and protected always.

This exercise is now completed.

Breathe deeply.

Mentally thank your angel, archangel and unicorn helpers for their support.

Thank Brigit for her strength, and her words of wisdom and deep healing.

Have a stamp of your feet, shake of your hands and maybe a wipe of your brow!

Back into reality, and maybe time for a breath of

fresh air or a cup of tea before you write your journal.

Well done.

You will be lighting-up the Heavens now with your Divine Torch.

CHAPTER SIX

Sacred Space and Self-Healing

What exactly is sacred space?

Different religions and belief systems have their own interpretations of what constitutes a 'sacred space'.

There are many books dedicated to this subject alone and so here I will merely scratch the surface and offer you the 'bare bones'!

In the last chapter we began to purify and cleanse ourselves. If we apply the same principles to our home, our environment and our work place then we can create our own sacred space. This is an area which we have purified and cleansed by removing negative energies and bringing in Love and Light, to create an area of peace, calm, harmony and healing.

Why do we need to create sacred space?

In this busy, fast-paced, hurly-burly, materialistic world of ours it is an absolute joy, and perhaps necessity, to have a place of peace and tranquillity that we can escape to when the need arises. This may be the safe haven of our home; it could be a park bench, the local church, or a snatched yoga class.

If we want to relax or involve ourselves in some spiritual pursuits, like meditation, reading, praying, writing or healing then to surround ourselves with positive energies in a special sacred place is the very best and most beneficial option.

Time to create a sacred space.

Where exactly can we create a sacred space?

Sacred space can be an *actual* physical place, a favourite stretch of beach, a corner of your garden, a river bank, your conservatory, your living-room or anywhere else that you can feel safe, secure and calm.

It may be that the only space available to you where you can be uninterrupted, alone and feel safe and secure is your **car**. Anywhere is fine. It's your sacred space, and your choice.

No rules. Perfect freedom.

If we have absolutely *nowhere* to create a special space for ourselves, or if a situation arises for us when we are miles away from our actual sacred space, then we can *visualise* a sacred space. This is every bit as good.

We could mentally picture ourselves in a setting in nature, by a waterfall we may have seen in a TV documentary, in a crystal cave from a previous meditation, a place from your dreams or on a tropical island. The sky is not the limit!

Let your imagination run free, and create yourself a beautiful sacred space.

Here's one I prepared earlier!

This is my own visualization of a sacred space, or cleansing sanctuary.

You are very welcome to join me there at any time!

Alternatively, you have the natural capacity to make a strong mental image or visualization of your own.

I can 'see' a cave made of amethyst and quartz crystals, with master crystal points at the opening. Some of the amethysts are of the deepest, clearest purple hue. Others are a delicate lavender colour, and the quartz is crystal clear.

There is a waterfall of pure spring water which washes through the cave, and down the slope into trees and forests beyond. There is a silver violet flame which removes any negativity from the water, and further downstream is a strip of smoky quartz which finally filters any particles of fear or negativity which remain.

Mother Earth will transform and transmute these into positive energy in her own wonderful ways.

Around the top of the cave stand two magnificent white peacocks, and all around the waterfall are a wave of majestic unicorns, and my power animals are by my side.

I remember the first time I visited here that it was a full moon, and the mysterious silvery light shone on myself and my friends and angels from the Angelic Kingdom.

'I will come here again', I thought to myself.

We can all create a sacred space almost anywhere.

E.g. If I am giving a talk, giving a healing session or running a workshop in a room, hall, or someone's home then I need to be able to create a sacred space wherever I may be. I will explain how I do this later in the chapter.

What exactly are the sacred spaces that are called sacred sites?

Some sacred spaces are actual sacred sites, and are recognised worldwide.

E.g. Stonehenge, Arbor Low, Machu Picchu, Ayers Rock, the Taj Mahal etc.

However, the most sacred of sacred sites could be your back garden or the local village hall!

It is my belief that all prayers, devotions, meditations or the like are equal, whether they are offered from a cardboard box or a cathedral, a public house or a pulpit, from the street or a sanctuary.

All the same to God and the universe wherever they come from, just the same.

If your intention to create a sacred space is pure in heart, then that is all that really matters, wherever you are.

Every religion and belief system has formulated and evolved their own rituals and procedures over many centuries to make their surroundings pure and blessed, and to prepare their participants for worship.

E.g. In some churches incense will be swung, prayers will be said, candles will be lit, and holy water will be used.

Experts in the ancient oriental art of Feng Shui will use specific methods to 'space clear' or to create sacred space. They will burn incense, light candles, sprinkle holy water, and offer prayers and flowers.

Druids may create a sacred circle, cast a circle/s, or prepare a sacred grove, from a group of trees, by 'smudging' (cleansing spiritually) the area by burning incense, spreading salt, lighting a candle or torch, creating a 'pool' of water in a bowl, and then they will dedicate this sacred space by a ceremony of words and invocations.

It is a profound and interesting concept to discover the commonality between such diverse belief systems from different sides of the world.

All use the natural elements to sanctify and purify their holy places to make them sacred:

- Air
- Water
- Fire and
- Earth.

The incense represents the element of air, water can be used in all its forms, fire is characterised by the use of a candle or torch, and earth is represented by the use of crystals, flowers, salt etc.

Water and Earth are recognised as the feminine elements, and Air and Fire as the masculine.

Interestingly, I draw something from all these different faiths when I create a sacred space myself. The very first time I spiritually prepared my 'space' for some healing sessions I intuitively used candles, crystals, incense and water. It was only afterwards that I realised that I was in actual fact using each of the four elements!

I must have tuned into some ancient wisdom and traditions psychically without even knowing.

How exactly can we create a sacred space in a public room, or strange location?

If I need to create a sacred space in a public room, prior to a spiritual workshop, then I would proceed as follows:

- First of all I protect myself spiritually, probably using The Christ Light.
- I mentally state my intentions, and ask for the support and guidance of the Angelic Kingdom of angels, archangels and unicorns.
- I may say, 'I am going to create a sacred space, here and now, and ask that all the participants, myself included, are protected and helped to understand and learn everything that we need to at the present time. I ask that we are surrounded by the Love and Light of the Angelic Kingdom, and that the ascended masters, guides, and power animals that we need to help us heal and learn join with us at this special and sacred time.'
- I would then walk around the perimeter of the room, and ask that the Angels of Purification and Archangel Gabriel purify the area, and remove any negative energy that may be present from previous occupants.
- I then ask that in each corner of the room, to the North, to the South, to the East and to the West stand a magnificent unicorn. Their horns point into the middle of the room, and from these radiant horns shines a pure white Light of the most intense and powerful kind.
- I then ask that in each of these positions are also the archangels.
- Archangel Michael to the North, bringing us ultimate protection, safety, truth, strength and courage, also representing the Earth.
- Archangel Uriel to the South, bringing us the Light of

God, illumination, peace, purification and creativity, also representing Fire.

- Archangel Raphael to the West, bringing us Love, healing, wisdom, unification and harmony, also representing Water.
- Archangel Gabriel to the East, bringing us communication from the Heavens, purification and inspiration, also representing Air.
- I may at this point also use my Balinese small cymbals, and 'ding' them together and wave them around a little! This uses sound as a 'back-up' purifier! I ask at the same time that any negative energy is removed, and transmuted by Mother Earth into positive ones for the benefit of mankind. This would complete my procedure and could be completed in as little as 5 minutes.

How exactly do these 4 elements 'work'?

Let's presume first of all that the area you have chosen is nice and clean, and de-cluttered.

We can use all of the elements of earth, water, air and fire in the purification process, as we have already discovered.

Each of them can cleanse and purify a particular space, room, building or whole area.

Purification by earth.

How on Earth can we purify by Earth?!

By using objects, e.g. crystals, flowers, floral essences, salt etc. from the earth, and that therefore represent earth energies we can connect with the ancient healing and the purification powers of Mother Earth.

If we ask for angelic and unicorn guidance and also trust in our own intuition we can then position the crystals etc. in the best possible positions to ensure high level energies in the area, and to absorb and remove any negative energies.

Maybe put them on a windowsill, or a mantelpiece. Wherever seems right, it is.

Some crystals commonly used to absorb negative energies, and for protection are smoky quartz, amethyst, carnelian, jet, tiger's eye, or indeed whichever crystal you feel attracted to use.

Go with your intuition!

If you do not own any crystals, or can't afford to buy any flowers, it's not a problem.

You could cut out pictures from old magazines, or draw the shape and colour of the crystal you are drawn to.

Children's marbles or pottery ornaments from a car-boot sale could represent Earth equally well. After all, the clay that pots are made from and the glass (silica) that marbles are formed out of are all from our own dear Mother Earth.

We should remember that each crystal has its own energy, and is also sensitive to other energies. Some crystals are powerful absorbers of negative energies, and so we need to look after them!

It is important to regularly 'cleanse' our crystals.

This re-energises them, and also washes away any negative energy.

There are different methods of cleansing but for the majority of crystals simply hold your crystal under cold running water whilst holding the thought of 'cleansing'.

There are many wonderful books available which will give more specific advice if necessary.

Never underestimate the power of a crystal however small it may be!

Purification by fire.

Fire is the only element that not only purifies, but at the same time remains pure itself.

Air, water and earth objects used in the purification process need either replacing or cleansing to remain effective.

E.g. Cleansing our crystals etc.

If it is inappropriate or unsafe to have an actual fire in the space then consider using candles instead, which are fire in miniature, and more manageable!

Candles can be ignited, and then ceremoniously dedicated for a specific purpose.

E.g. You could say,

'In lighting this candle I ask that this sacred space remains pure and that this small light brings comfort and warmth to all who see it.'

Fire has been used in religious ceremonies since early man, and the early shamanic rituals would have been carried out around a fire, in a sacred circle.

We could ask the goddess of fire and sun, the ancient Celtic warrior goddess Brigit, to help us in our purification by fire. She is a triple goddess of the flame, highly appropriate, and these manifestations of fire help to purify us and our environment, promote healing and increase our creativity and fertility.

We met her in the last chapter, and here she is again, bringing her powerful energy to help us once more.

She will come in a flash of flame!

Purification by air.

We humans have very sensitive noses and sense of smell. It goes without saying that if we have an objectionable smell, e.g. rotting fish, sewage etc. in an area this will not enhance the sacredness or purity!

Air quality is therefore very important in an area of home or work environment.

An incense stick being burnt will immediately lift the spirit, sweeten the air and purify the atmosphere.

Used in the same way aromatic oils have the same beneficial effect. Some healers will use smudge sticks to purify an area and remove negative energies. Shamans and those using the ways of the North American Native traditions will also smudge themselves to cleanse their aura, and will also smudge others to rid any negative energy.

Smudge sticks are held in the hand, made of dried herbs and are burnt and used like incense sticks.

Incense sticks are readily available in many shops now, and are not too expensive. Some aromatic oil is very costly, but a little does go a long way!

Purification by water.

No problems with cost here!

How lucky we are to have an immediate source of clean drinkable water on tap!

Natural spring water has powerful healing properties, and can be used to bath, to wash, to clean, and also to drink!

Some wells of spring water have become sacred sites, and have attracted pilgrims to 'take the waters' for thousands of years.

E.g. The Chalice Well, at the foot of the Glastonbury Tor, has been honoured as a sacred site for many, many hundreds of years, and has attracted many visitors to taste its pure waters for purification, healing and well-being.

I personally cleansed my healing crystals in the Chalice Well gardens in the water as it poured out of the Lion's Head. They sparkled and shone, and I am convinced are vibrating at a higher level, and also healing at a deeper and more profound level.

Powerful stuff this H2O.

We can sprinkle water which we have blessed, by a simple invocation, around the area.

Such as:

'I ask that this water brings health, healing and happiness to this sacred space that I have created. Thank you to the Angels of the West who look after all the areas of water in the world, the oceans, seas, rivers, lakes, streams and sacred wells.'

When we work to create a sacred space with the beautiful elements of Mother Earth we are connecting with the ancient wisdom and traditions of those spiritual beings and our ancestors who lived long ago, and who help us now in our endeavours to help heal ourselves, Mother Earth and the planet.

How exactly can we create a sacred space in our own home?

If you are fortunate enough to have an area in your home or environment that you can dedicate permanently as sacred space then you are truly blessed.

It may be a small corner of your living-room, or a windowsill, or an even larger area of your garden, or even the shed!

You may want to place crystals there, feathers that you have found, fossils collected on a special beach (with wonderful memories maybe), flowers, stones, twigs, candles, photographs, shells, pictures, angel or Tarot cards, wands, angel confetti, ornaments or whatever else that you have collected, and touches and feeds your soul.

If you are unable to find a special place for all these items then you may consider buying a beautiful box to keep them in, a very sacred container.

In the Druid tradition a Druidess will keep her treasures from nature in her 'crane bag', a special carrier for her prized possessions.

I hope that you enjoy creating your own sacred space, and that it gives you peace, and most importantly brings you closer to inner peace.

Is 'space clearing' the same as creating sacred space?

Feng Shui is an ancient oriental art or method of purifying an area.

The belief is that our actual environment, where we

live and where we work, plays a most crucial part of our quest to increase our personal spiritual energy levels.

I agree with them.

Feng Shui practitioners dedicate a lifetime to their craft, and learning methods of creating sacred space, and space clearing for our houses and places of work.

It is my understanding that space clearing and creating sacred space are broadly speaking the same procedure.

The words 'feng' and 'shui' in Chinese, interpret as 'wind' and 'water'.

These are the two forces of natural energy.

A quotation from ancient China says

'If there is harmony in the home,
there will be order in the nation.
If there is order in the nation,
there will be peace in the world.'

Powerful words and powerful energies!

There are many and varied books on this subject, if you wish to learn more about the art of this ancient practise of enhancing and harmonising the flow of energy in your surroundings.

One of the most effective, therapeutic and powerful Feng Shui procedures is 'Clearing Clutter'.

This is also a very powerful way of clearing out negatives in a more literal sense!

Clearing cupboards etc.

A practical purification exercise.

Anything which does not serve any purpose whatsoever in your life is clutter.

If, unfortunately, you are thinking here about a fellow human being who seems to have limited use or to not play a useful part in your life, that is a different dilemma, and not part of this particular exercise!

This is a very physical, practical, down-to-Earth activity.

Anything that you have in your home and are not using is clutter.

Perhaps de-clutter one drawer to start with, or if you are relatively clutter free begin in one room. Dependent on how much clutter that you have accumulated this project could be a one hour job, one day, one week, or keep you going for the next year!

If you thoroughly de-clutter one single drawer you will almost certainly feel the benefits immediately. You may also have a rather smug expression!

You have taken a lifetime to accumulate this baggage.

It is an important step towards a lighter YOU and may take time.

The negative draining energy which builds up, and stagnates in cluttered areas, is almost tangible.

When energy moves it is alive, vibrant, clear, clean and healthy.

Clearing clutter moves energy.

The therapeutic effect is amazing.

You will feel energised, empowered and lighter in every way.

A very dear friend of mine says, 'You can't make omelettes without breaking eggs.'…in other words it may look worse before it gets better!

Most importantly, moving clutter and rubbish out of your life makes a sacred space for new brighter energies to come into your life.

The angels, archangels and unicorns will love the new atmosphere, and will be queuing up to make their presence felt.

If any of your clutter can be recycled, or donated to charity shops, so much the better.

Other people will then benefit from this energy release as much as you.

Keep up your water intake, it helps with the purification process, and with all this hard work we don't want you dehydrating!

There are other ways to purify an area spiritually, as follows;

Sound as a purifier.

We can also use **sound**. This can be as simple as playing a CD of relaxing music in the background. More active methods are shaking rattles or banging drums to disperse negative energies.

Clapping hands together in corners of a room is also very effective, and breaks up stagnant areas of energy build-up. If you feel inclined to sing or chant this can be a beautiful way to uplift and purify an area.

However, if you are tone deaf, like me, perhaps use the other methods. Unless you are on your own, in which case… Go for it!

Well, go for it anyway!

What else can help to create a sacred space?

We can use symbols, shapes, colours, pictures, ornaments, fabrics and drapes and so the list goes on.

In a spiritual 'nutshell' we can say that:

Shapes and colours all can be used to enhance a sacred space.

Circles, squares and triangles each have their own particular energies.

Colours have individual energies, and will maximise a purification ceremony in some cases.

E.g. Lapis Lazuli blue can symbolise Mary Magdalene energy, and purple is accepted to be a highly spiritual colour.

As with all this information…Use your own intuition. Do what seems the right thing for you.

We can all create a sacred space for ourselves wherever and whenever we want or need to.

All we really need is the intention, and then we can create an area of PEACE out of thin air, and sacred space at the drop of a hat.

A very dramatic thought, rather a cliché, but magical indeed!

Talking of magic and drama, the unicorns are awaiting the next step of our journey with them…self-healing.

This is bringing the peace of your sanctuary or sacred space into your very being…Inner Peace.

The Angelic Kingdom is delighted to help you, and awaits your call.

We can purify our environment and we can purify and heal ourselves, and by transmuting negative energies into positive ones, and by working on the purification of ourselves and our environment we raise our personal energy levels to a higher spiritual level.

This in turn raises the energy of the planet, and brings us ever nearer to the days of Heaven on Earth.

Know that the unicorns are happy for us to harness their magical master-healing energies to bring self-healing to ourselves at the deep level of the soul.

Know that the Angelic Kingdom of angels, archangels and unicorns will help us to purify, cleanse and heal ourselves in the sacred space which we have created.

Let the magic continue...

EXERCISE SIX

Self-healing with the Unicorns.

We know that the energy of a unicorn is

- Pure
- Undiluted and powerful
- High-vibrational
- High-energy
- High-frequency and
- Transformational.

We know that they want to help us to heal at the deep level of the soul.

We know that they are master-healers, and will use their magic and mystery to help us produce miracles of self-healing.

A very powerful and positive outcome is in store for you as you meet your own special and sacred unicorn in this exercise.

Then let's begin...

You may consider working with a friend for this section. One of you could read the meditation to the other, and then swap over. Alternatively you could tape the words so that you can concentrate completely on the session.

This self-healing comes in two parts.

In the first part you are going to create your own sacred space, using any or all of the methods in this chapter which feel right for you at this time.

The second part is a self-healing meditation at the deep level of the soul. It is important to choose a time for this healing session when you feel relaxed and when you will be uninterrupted.

Part One.

Start to create your own sacred space. Take as much time as you need.

When you feel that you are ready and prepared you can now begin to focus on your breathing. Start to relax and breathe deeply.

Know that you are totally protected and loved in this special sacred space that you have created.

When you feel ready you can begin to concentrate on deepening your breathing and move gently into the following words of the meditation...

Part Two.

Focus on your breathing. Breathing slowly and deeply.

Take a moment now to call in your usual trusted spiritual friends, guides, angels, your guardian angel, your power animals and your own special and sacred unicorn.

Know that you are grounded and protected as you embark on this loving journey of soul-healing towards deeper wisdom and greater understanding.

Know that you are loved in this sacred healing space, and know that you are safe and secure, surrounded and protected by your chosen helpers.

Feel your body relax, your muscles warm and soft, your shoulders dropped and without tension, your legs and arms are feeling heavy and soft.

Know that your feet are touching the floor and you are grounded to Mother Earth, safe and secure.

With each breath you feel calmer, more relaxed and more peaceful and you feel more loved than ever before.

Your breathing is steady and deep and your body is warm and relaxed.

Trust and know that you have all the love and support that you need from the Angelic Kingdom.

Breathing in, imagine a beautiful, healing, warm, loving, golden light coming down from the heavens and filling every cell, bone and pore of your body with the healing warmth and loving light of this powerful golden colour.

Breathe in even more of this golden light and now imagine it filling your heart and heart chakra, touching your very soul.

Place your hand on your heart and sense the deep connection with your inner light, your Divine centre, your inner spark, your highest consciousness, your SOUL, your Divine self, YOU.

That part of you which has been with you forever, and will live forever, is immortal and will never die, your SOUL.

Connect with that place, your sacred self, your sacred soul centre and fill it with love and light. Open your heart.

Take a few moments to relax in this sacred space which you have created and know that you can return to this place of peace and tranquillity at any time and enjoy this sacred connection with your soul.

Thank your soul for being you and know that your soul brings forward your great qualities, your amazing gifts and thank your soul for all the positive life lessons it has provided for you to gain wisdom on your road to enlightenment.

Breathe deeply. Know that you are safe and secure.

Now is the time to call on your OWN special unicorn, to ask him or her to come to your side, invite them to join you, and walk beside you and to lead you forwards on this soul journey towards healing. Mentally call the unicorn to you now.

This unicorn may be an old friend that you remember from the Golden days of Atlantis. He could be young and playful, she may be old and wise but this is your OWN unicorn, your special spiritual friend.

Take a few moments to open your heart to this magical being, introduce yourselves and connect your souls for the road ahead.

Let them help you to harness their magical and

majestic power for yourself, on this special spiritual journey towards enlightenment, self-fulfilment, acceptance, love and approval of yourself in this soul-healing. They can bring peace and purity into your life.

They are so warm and gentle, and fill you with tenderness and you feel enveloped with harmony, joy and well-being.

Take this opportunity to embrace the pure, powerful and loving energy of your own magical unicorn. Open your heart to the love they bring you.

Call on your unicorn to be a bridge to healing and to empower you to believe in yourself and love yourself enough to heal and move on in your life.

Let them help you to harness their power for yourself.

Let them lead you to the healing which your soul is crying out for.

Let them use their radiant horn to pinpoint the source of any deep-rooted pain, negative thoughts, repressed anger, unresolved childhood issues of abandonment, rejection, abuse and anxiety, guilt, shame, fear, phobias and the like.

Let them pierce the pain and allow it to release painlessly and permanently in a wonderfully positive, pure and simple way.

Claim the life you were born to live.

Let the healing energies of the unicorns gallop and race through your veins; empowering, cleansing, healing, nourishing and bringing you ever nearer to your full potential and your soul purpose as a wonderful human-being.

Let their healing energies find the sweet centre of your loving heart, to touch you deeply, to remove the barriers of fear, distrust, unrequited love, an abused childhood or violent partnership or the like from around your wounded heart.

Let the love of the Universe into your very being, healing, caressing, mending and repairing this centre of your life, your heart and soul.

Let the love of the Divine bring new meaning, peace, balance, harmony, dignity, innocence and purity into your mind, body and soul.

Let the unicorn touch you and reawaken the love, trust, self-belief and self-esteem that you may have forgotten or frozen out.

Feel your body respond to the warmth and heat of this love which fills your very being, and removes all the barriers that you may have placed around your heart and soul.

Let them melt away in love and peace.

Know that you now feel lighter, you feel free and you are liberated. The unicorn energy brings you FREEDOM.

Know now that you are a pure being of Love and Light.

Your soul is cleansed, revitalized, reformed and rebalanced.

You are a pure being, lighter, brighter and more healed than ever before.

Accept and love yourself.

You are a beautiful soul in a beautiful body,

Love this day and remember this healing;

Know that this is the start of your new life

To inspire and heal others,

To teach and guide others,

To motivate and mentor others.

This is your life

This is your destiny

This is your mission

This is your purpose

This is your path and your journey

This is your Divine road to enlightenment and illumination and

Peace on Earth for yourself and others.

Feel the love and power your unicorn brings you now and also in the future.

Know that your unicorn will help you forgive and forget those people who may have hurt you in your past.

Know that you have survived the pain of the past, and are beginning to heal, and are moving ever closer towards your own highest personal potential, and closer to illumination and enlightenment.

Enjoy this magical connection and know that you can reconnect with this spiritual friend at any time.

Thank your angel helpers, and anyone else who has supported you during this self-healing session.

Open your eyes, and return to waking consciousness.

How do you feel?

Hopefully, you will feel lighter and unburdened as you have released some negativity from your home, your environment and more importantly YOURSELF!

Time for you to write up your journal. Maybe time for a cup of tea.

You deserve it!

CHAPTER SEVEN

The Ten Keys

Now you are ready to take the next big steps towards the rest of your life!

There are ten keys to open the 'master-door' of your being to bring you closer to the answers to the eternal mysteries of life, and bring you adventure, confidence, passion and peace of mind.

Ten keys to unlock your potential and personal power to bring you to your soul purpose, positivity and to LIGHT UP YOUR LIFE!

When you have mastered each key it is like a step on a ladder to freedom.

Ten steps to the freedom to fly and your passport to the stars!

Each key has its own spiritual meaning and its own channelled affirmation or message/s which usually start/s, 'Know that…', but any of the text in italics is also the key to distinct 'channelled' words.

The keys do not have to be turned in a particular order but, just like the numbered dials in a combination lock, each key has to be mastered, all ten, before the master-door swings open.

When the final key is fathomed then the mysteries

become clear and are finally understood and illuminated forever.

The skies light up
Stars shoot across the heavens
A circle of Light is ignited
And burns through the night sky
In a shimmering burst of
Pure white light
A soul is awakened
And shown to the world,
That's YOU!

Some of the keys are easier to turn than others.

Some of the keys will be resistant, set in their ways and difficult to shift.

This is normal, and it would be unrealistic to expect otherwise.

God, the Universe and your spiritual friends know when you are trying to achieve something new, or to break a recurring pattern in your life, or to release a negative thought that you may have been generating for decades.

They will make allowances for us, and help us to turn the key.

We are not, and never will be a **perfected soul** on this Earth plane.

If we move in the right direction, have the intention to change and transform, then the powers that be will acknowledge this and can bestow an element of grace on us.

They can take over the problem and difficult area for us and sort it out.

No key will be left unturned if we genuinely want to learn the lesson.

The key will magically unlock and not bar our progress.

Some of these occurrences are due to the mysterious workings of God.

As it says in one of the Olney Hymns of 1779:

'God moves in a mysterious way

His wonders to perform;

He plants His footsteps in the sea,

And rides upon the storm.'

Some may be called MIRACLES!

(And yes) When we are talking about mysteries, magic and miracles that's when the majestic unicorns rise up to their fullest height, with their radiant horns touching the heavens, and shine their golden-white light of illumination upon us.

They are never out of the picture for long.

After all, this book is dedicated to them!

And YOU!

Now to the keys…

KEY 1.

Bring in the heavy gang!
In other words, ask the Lightworkers to help you.
'Know that you are supported.'

We can ask the Angelic Kingdom to assist us and they will be delighted to help.

There are hosts of angels to help us, whenever we need them.

This is a day and night service. We can call on our angelic helpers at any time, and know that they will come immediately.

We each have our very own guardian angel. They are with us from the moment of conception, to the moment we have passed successfully into the world of spirit at the end of each lifetime.

They do not abandon us if we are tempted by the dark side, or lose sight of our path or go off the rails.

They are with us all the way, whatever path we choose. However we act or behave, whether we are drunk and disorderly or prim and proper!

They are by our side, no matter what. Their love for us is unconditional.

Your guardian angel is stuck with you!

They have no freewill, and are committed to walk with you, to support and guide you, to reassure and protect you, and to love you unconditionally, whatever you get up to!

Unicorns are slightly different, as you will have discovered.

They are from the Angelic Kingdom, it's true, and give us the same unconditional love.

However, it seems that they have been given a free rein in this area! They can come and go as they wish, as they have been given Divine freedom, just like ourselves.

They can gallop into our life in a flash, walk beside us

for as long as it takes, but they can go again as quickly as they came.

The whole of the Angelic Kingdom have the power and desire to shower unconditional love on each and every one of us.

There are also angels with specific, specialised strengths and area of particular expertise.

E.g. Angels of Purification

Angels of Healing

Angels of Ascension

Angels of Transformation

Angels of Transmutation and angels who will assist us in every aspect of our lives.

If you are not quite sure of the name of the angel who you need to ask for, just mentally ask for the angel who can help you the most at this time.

This will be most effective, almost like an angel Yellow Pages!

The Angelic Kingdom of angels, archangels, and unicorns give us the greatest gift of all...their UNCONDITIONAL LOVE.

The greatest lesson for our soul to learn, which is also the hardest, is to try to love ourselves and each other unconditionally.

When we have mastered this we will shine with the golden-white light of an ascended and awakened soul.

This is a love without any conditions and without any strings attached!

This is a love of purity and simplicity,

This is a love which is uncomplicated, deep and powerful,
This is a love which touches the soul, and ignites passion,
Passion is the energy of the soul.
This is a love which is not just for birthdays or Christmas,
or days of grief and sadness,
This is a love 24/7, for now and always!
Unconditional Love.

We always have the love and support of the Angelic Kingdom, particularly the unicorns and also our other spiritual friends, ancestors, guides, power animals, ascended masters, saints, the goddesses and our soul family, seen and unseen.

KEY 1...BRING IN THE HEAVY GANG! ASK THE LIGHTWORKERS TO HELP YOU!!

KEY 2

Put yourself in the driving seat!
THIS IS YOUR LIFE!
You have rights,
You have power,
You have both blessings and challenges,
You have the opportunity to do anything,
And go anywhere!!
Claim your power,
Take the wheel,
And drive,
Take control.
This is a journey like no other,
And will bring you happiness and fulfilment,

This is a journey to excavate your true self,
Bring yourself to the LIGHT,
Unearth yourself and
**EMERGE AS THE SHINING STAR
OF LOVE AND LIGHT
THAT YOU WERE BORN TO BE!**
The journey that we take is special and unique to each
of us.

No-one travels the same path,
We each have different lessons to learn,
Challenges to face, and changes to consider,
Some of us will seem to have the easier route,
And others chosen the road less travelled,
More rocky with many pitfalls along the way,
We may have learnt not to compare,
Things are not as straightforward as they may seem.
Whether we are healthy, wealthy and wise
Or ill, poverty-stricken and uneducated,
The opportunities will be given to us all,
To face up to the situations our soul has drawn to us
And find the jewel within us all,
Our sweet heart centre
and unconditional love.

***

When you were young, you were not in control; you
may have had no voice and no power. Others may have
come and taken over your life and taken control over
you.

They may have taken the 'wheel' of your 'car' and taken you to places that you did not want to go.

Now you can put yourself in the driver's seat.

Or to say it in another way, with the unicorns in mind, now you can take the reins!

If we choose the positive road, or the right track, then the universe will work with us and bring positive people, places and events into our lives.

God is the ultimate creator, but if we accept our own power and our own divinity we realise that we can co-create our future.

Remember,

You are in control of this 'car'.

You have a choice where to go.

You are in the driver's seat.

You have free will and freedom.

You can go wherever you want to go.

If you want to go really fast: call in the unicorns!

They will also walk beside you if you need to feel your feet and move slowly.

Plus, they will bring the wonderful mixture of

1. Energy – the fuel!
2. Direction – the Sat Nav. of the Angelic Kingdom!
3. Focus – Where do I want to go?
4. Passion – the energy of the soul and
5. Purity – they lighten the load, and remove the 'baggage'!

'Know that the time is right
Know that you are loved,

128

Know that you are where you are meant to be,

Know that there are no wrong roads, no mistakes, only learning.'

KEY 2... PUT YOURSELF IN THE DRIVING SEAT!

KEY 3

Throw away all your negative thought 'video tapes'!

They really don't work anymore.

We all have them, the voice on our shoulder or the negative thought running in our head that tells us in a spectacular fashion what are our shortcomings and failures.

These 'tapes' may have been playing on a continuous loop for decades and we still may believe them.

Now is the time to stop listening to these tapes. They are indeed obsolete!

Try to identify one of the negative thoughts that you have about yourself that you know can pop into your head at any time.

Maybe you have been told so often that you are stupid that you believe it.

Try and catch that thought, either now or when you think it again.

We have approximately 60,000 thoughts a day, so you will, unfortunately, have several hundred negative thoughts to deal with.

Some typical 'tapes' may have the following messages:

'You are ugly'/ 'I am ugly'

'You are fat'/ 'I am fat'
'You can't sing'/ 'I can't sing'
'You don't like vegetables'/ 'I don't like vegetables'
'No-one will ever love you'/ 'I am unlovable'
'You can't trust anyone'/ 'I can't trust anyone'
'The world is a dangerous place'/ 'I am unsafe'
'You can't manage money'/ 'I am useless with money'
etc.

You can 'catch' these thoughts and self-doubts and identify the 'tapes' and throw them away!

A good place to throw them is onto 'Brigit's Fire Wheel' the purification exercise we used at the end of Chapter 5.

Time to change and clear all those negative thoughts out of your life.

Another method to use to remove them is to try to hang on to the next negative thought you have about yourself, take a deep breath, ask for your angelic support, put yourself in the driver's seat and ask yourself the following questions:

- Who said it to you first?
- Can you remember when it was?
- Do you believe it?
- Where are you feeling it (in your body)?
- Does it have a colour?
- Does it have a shape?

Try to put your hand on the place where you are feeling

the reaction in your body to this negative thought about yourself.

If it has a colour already, try and imagine what colour you would **prefer** it to be.

When you have decided on this preferred colour, you can proceed with this colour-healing process as follows:

- ZAP the spot with your chosen colour
- Imagine the original colour draining away, down your body, dissolving and disappearing as it goes down your legs and then out of your body and into Mother Earth who will work her magic and transform it into positive energy again.

Goodbye to this negative thought.

What colour is the area now?

Do you still believe the negative thought?

If so you can repeat the exercise again. Maybe, consider using a different colour.

If you discover very traumatic or painful thoughts and memories do not be afraid to seek medical advice or counselling etc.

You can reinforce this removal of the negative thoughts you have discovered in this next supplementary exercise, which is supremely successful.

Write them down on a piece of paper, and then safely and therapeutically **shred** them.

Even more therapeutically you could then ceremoniously **burn** the shredded paper!

This healing is wonderfully cleansing and very powerful.

It's time to release these damaging and self-limiting negative thoughts and time for a positive change.

'Know that if we do what we've always done we get what we've always got!'

KEY 3...THROW AWAY ALL YOUR NEGATIVE THOUHT 'VIDEO TAPES'!

KEY 4.

It's not me, it's them!
Or, in other words, don't take anything personally.

If we are sensitive to the opinions and judgements of others then we empower them to make us either happy or sad by their comments.

We become 'reactors' and disempower ourselves.

If we can instead become 'creators' we build our own lives in the knowledge that the attitudes, actions, accusations and opinions of others will not stop us becoming the person we are destined to be!

Believe in yourself,

Trust in your own worth.

'Know that other people have their own issues and can project them onto others. This is their 'stuff' and nothing to do with you.'

'Know that you are strong and the comments and actions of others cannot either destroy or empower your soul.'

'Know that you create your world.'

'Know that you always have a choice.'
'Know that you can dance to your own tune.'
'Know that you are a beautiful soul inside and out.'
'Know that the words and actions of others
Can only hurt you if you choose to let them!'

It is your journey, to find out that the person who needs to love you the most, who is very close to you, maybe doesn't know you very well, but that person is YOU!

It will be those people who seek to humiliate, ridicule, abuse, torment and try to demean you that bring you the greatest challenges.

You are a mirror to their soul.

They see something in you which they do not like, or even recognise about themselves.

Interestingly, it is these same people that we draw towards us, and into our lives that are the soul-friends who bring us the greatest soul GIFTS in the midst of their hardest challenge.

The lesson which we need to learn from them is to face up to ourselves, not to take criticisms personally, and try to find the way to love ourselves, warts and all!

KEY 4…IT'S NOT ME, IT'S THEM!

KEY 5

Learn to say NO!

'Know that you do not have to do anything that you don't want to.'

'Know that you have a choice.'

'Know that you are not responsible for the lives and happiness of others.'***

*** Unless you have small children or elderly parents!

'Know that you can forget the "I really should do that" syndrome.'

'Know that you are in control of your own life.'

Learn to say NO!

It is not rude, impolite, disrespectful or uncaring to say 'No', it is your **right**.

Sometimes it is easier to have resolve and steadfastness if we set our own 'boundaries' or what we are happy to do, and then try to stick to them.

Then we know exactly what we will or will not do for love or anything else.

In other words, do not have an open 'rucksack' on your shoulders for others to put in their own problems and troubles. Listen and empathise but try not to take on the burdens of others and close your 'rucksack'.

We all know the saying, 'I seem to have the weight of the world on my shoulders.'

LEARN TO SAY NO!

Maybe you're thinking that's easier said than done.

If the thought of saying no to someone close to you makes you feel physically sick, frightened, panicky or fills you with dread then please do not say no to them but instead ask yourself the following questions:

Is this person a bully?

Is this person abusing me in some way?

Does this person 'control' me?

Am I happy with this situation?

Does this person respect and value my feelings and opinions?

Sometimes, we need help to give us the courage to say no to someone. Perhaps you may consider having some counselling or therapy to boost your self-confidence and self-worth.

We can be bullied or abused physically, mentally, verbally and indeed spiritually.

The real truth about a person or a situation close to us can be hard to bear.

We may find it easier to live under the illusion of excuses and lie to ourselves about the reality.

Your mind can fool you, but your body will always speak the truth!

Do you have any medical problems, for example disturbed sleep or insomnia, stress headache or migraine, or upset stomach or irritable bowel syndrome?

Could there be an underlying reason for this illness?

Relax and ask your soul for the answer you seek.

At the deep level of our soul we know all the answers, but sometimes the truth is hard to bear.

Certainly when we have turned the previous keys we will have brought some **changes** into our life. After these transformations comes the **challenge** of this key 5, to learn to say no.

As your self-worth and confidence in yourself increases then those significant others in your life will notice the difference!

They may struggle to accept these changes and try to reverse you to the earlier model!

They may try to knock you off track.

It was an easier journey for them when you were compliant and said yes to everything.

If you start to say no, even in a very respectful, pleasant and polite way, then you may hear the following,

'If you really loved me you would do it.'

'You used to be more fun.'

'Why are you being so mean and nasty?'

'You always used to do that and you never refused before.'

'If you were a good mother you would definitely help me.'

This can be a hard key to master, and if you are finding it difficult then the more important a 'key stage' it is for your journey.

If you are not sure whether you want to say no or not then ask yourself the following questions:

Do I feel as if I am trying to push water uphill?

Does doing this make my heart feel heavy?

Do I have to keep this a secret from my friends and family?

Does this bring me closer to my Divine purpose or mission in my life?

Does my soul cry out in pain when I do this?

Is this something that I really want to be doing?

Do I feel safe to say no next time?

Do I need to seek help to deal with this?

Remember that you are not alone, and that the Angelic Kingdom wants to help you in all your spiritual endeavours towards illumination and enlightenment.

There are many helping agencies, counsellors and therapists to help you if you need it to assert your right to say no.

KEY 5... LEARN TO SAY NO!

KEY 6

Feed the 'Light' wolf.

There is a Native American parable which goes like this:

It is called The Battle of the wolves.

A Native American grandfather was talking to his grandson about how he felt.

He said,

'I feel as if I have two wolves fighting in my heart.

One wolf is the vengeful, angry, violent one.

The other wolf is the loving, compassionate one.'

The grandson asked him,

'Which wolf will win the fight in your heart?'

The grandfather answered,

'The one I feed.'

This seems to perfectly symbolise the soul, with its Light side and its dark side.

If we can feed our Light side, then we feed our soul.

It is not always easy. If someone is making our life hell then it is very difficult to send them Light. We must try to remember that if we attack them verbally or retaliate in any way then we are then in fact feeding our own dark wolf.

We must try to rise above it, take the moral higher ground, turn the other cheek and feed our lighter wolf.

'Know that you know how to do this.'

KEY 6... FEED THE 'LIGHT' WOLF!

KEY 7

Only compare downwards!

There is an anonymous saying, which goes like this:

'I cried because I had no shoes until I saw a man who had no feet.'

Sometimes we feel hard done by, as if life is unfair and we can think that others seem to have more than we do. However, if we compare **downwards** it not only makes us feel better, but also encourages us to feel more compassionate towards those in a worse state than ourselves.

It is easy to compare our life to that of others and to think the 'If only' syndrome!

I.e. Life would be different IF ONLY...

I was beautiful

I had lots of money

I lived in a big house

I didn't have to work

I was married to a wonderful person

I hadn't been abused

I was clever etc. etc.

This syndrome is a flawed, 'victim' speak, cop-out, an excuse or an easy excuse for us to avoid the truth of the matter.

The reality seems to be that it doesn't matter what you've got, it is who you are that matters.

Beauty, money, possessions, designer clothes, jewels, brains etc. are valuable indeed.

But it is the UNCONDITIONAL LOVE which we seek of ourselves and to give and receive from others which is PRICELESS!

The poorest people are those whose only wealth can be measured by their possessions.

We are a special and unique soul, and we have our own special and unique path to walk, and our individual lessons to learn and our own 'keys' to turn!

'Know that this is your life and that you are a beautiful soul.'

Live your life to the best that you can.

Try to reach your highest potential whatever the trials and tribulations that you have to endure.

They are the jewels to find on your path to wearing your own crown of illumination and spiritual majesty, your halo of the brightest Light.

KEY 7... ONLY COMPARE DOWNWARDS!!

KEY 8

Notice the 'mole-hills'!

Engage all your senses.

All six of them!

See, hear, touch, smell, feel and the sixth being the spiritual sense of 'knowing' or intuition.

When we are aware of our spiritual path then we become more aware of synchronicity, or the power and meaning of the apparent coincidence of spiritual signs.

Sometimes, we need to be silent and look for these signs. They may come in the form of a dream, a song, a bird, your surroundings, a chance meeting or even a 'mole-hill'.

What on Earth is a 'mole-hill'?

Literally, a mole-hill is little mound of soil cast up by a mole. Both unwanted and unexpected blots on the landscape!

This could be a sure sign that although everything was looking fine on the surface that there is certainly a lot of activity underground. Spiritually speaking it could be said that there is something coming up to the Light to be dealt with.

We need to notice these 'mole-hills' that may pop-up into our well-ordered and well-manicured life.

What is the lesson we need to learn?

Time to look beneath the surface,

Time to unearth those buried memories or scars on our soul,

Time to excavate and bring our true self to the Light of day.

What are we not seeing?

Noticing a 'mole-hill' is a sure sign that there is something we need to deal with and we cannot ignore it any longer.

If we fail to investigate our little 'mole-hill' then they will multiply and certainly get much bigger!

If we overlook it any longer then the 'issue' grows and grows until we may be dealing with a spiritual 'volcano'.

Anything can be a message from the world of spirit or an omen for your future.

Be observant and be aware!

We have lessons to learn on this human journey of ours. If we fail to notice the signs then we have to wait for the consequences.

In other words, until we learn the lesson that our soul valiantly keeps drawing towards us, the message will become bigger and bigger and the challenge harder and harder.

We will keep repeating the same pattern of our behaviour until we get the message.

At this point our soul will breathe a sigh of relief and think thank goodness for that!

Some of us learn the lesson easier than others.

Some will only need a small alarm-clock to 'wake them up' to the pursuit of the happiness, inner peace and fulfilment of the spiritual journey.

Whereas others may need dynamite under the bed and a tape of Big-Ben ringing in their ears to wake them up.

We are all different.

We are all special and unique.

Some of us will see the mole-hills and others will have to wait for the volcanos!

Our soul needs to know that we love ourselves unconditionally and it will help us all the way by bringing us soul-lessons, however painful they may be that we need to learn.

We will keep repeating the same patterns, suffering a recurring illness, having the same worrying thought about something we are doing, a nagging doubt about a 'friend', making the same mistakes, and drawing similar people into our lives until we see the signs and get the message.

It is our soul-journey to find the most important lesson and most beautiful gift of all…

TO LOVE OURSELVES UNCONDITIONALLY.

We can fool our minds, but our bodies tell the truth.

If we have ignored some health problem, and not heard the whispers of our soul, then the illness will unfortunately become more serious until we face up to it and seek out the appropriate treatment or therapy.

Some illnesses can point to the lessons the soul wishes us to learn.

E.g. Migraines can be the body's answer to being overworked and not saying no. Just like a computer which will crash when it is overloaded, the body's safety valve can be the onset of a migraine. Then the body has no choice but to stop. If we had listened to the whispers we could have slowed down, taken a break and avoided the pain.

If we give ourselves the time and space to listen for the whispers and to observe our surroundings we will be living in the magic of our lives.

Notice the mole-hills…those things which come up in your life which you would be sensible not to ignore!

The spiritual gifts which we learn in this University of life can never be lost, stolen or bought.

'The gifts of the soul are presents for life.'
KEY 8...NOTICE THE 'MOLE-HILLS'!

KEY 9

It could be a lot worse!
> **BE GRATEFUL!**

Believe me, it could be a lot worse.

Try to remember to give thanks every day to God, the Universe, the angels, the archangels, the unicorns, our ancestors, spirit guides, power animals, ascended masters, the elemental kingdom, goddesses, our friends, family, pets and our soul-friends and family and anyone else who you are blessed to have in your life.

However bad things seem for you at the moment try to be thankful for what is positive in your life.

Even if it is a very small thing, be grateful.

Gratitude is the answer to turn around the pain of negativity into the joy of positivity.

Practise every day giving thanks.

We seem to find it difficult to be grateful. If someone gives us an unexpected gift,

'You shouldn't have,' or

'I'm sorry I haven't got anything for you.'

Try to be grateful, and not immediately think of a negative motive for the gift!

'They must be feeling guilty. What have they done?' or

'What do they want?'

This could be unconditional love in action! Accept it.

KEY 9...IT COULD BE A LOT WORSE!

KEY 10

Be true to yourself!
'Know that you are loved, unconditionally,
Know that you can create your own future,
Know that you have made no mistakes, only learning
Know that you are a powerful and positive
Force for good in the world
Know that your Light brings illumination
To yourself and the Universe.'

If we can be true to ourselves, and true to others, it encourages joy and peace within ourselves.

Inner peace is perhaps one of the biggest gifts of all.

Every lie you make is a confession to yourself and the world
That you do not approve of what you have done,
Or who you are,
It is a wound to your soul,
It denies your authentic self,
It destroys your integrity,
It breaks and crumbles the foundations of who you are.
To lie is to feed the darkness and cast shadows
On your true being of Love and Light.
It is poisonous and kills relationships
And the TRUTH of whom you are.
To learn to say no is to understand
How to be true to yourself,
And speak your truth in a clear voice.
It is honest and gives you integrity and honour.

The foundations of a life well lived,
And a soul dancing to the tune of truth and integrity.

Be true to yourself!

Dance to your own tune not someone else's,

Celebrate your differences,

Accept your foibles!

Forgive yourself.

Sometimes there is a price to pay for someone or something.

Is it worth it?

Do you kill part of yourself and your soul by doing it?

Are you paying too high a price?

'Know that the truth will set you free.'

KEY 10...BE TRUE TO YOURSELF.

To recall the ten keys they are as follows...try and see if you can remember them.

Key One – Bring in the heavy gang!
Key Two – Put yourself in the driving seat!
Key Three – Throw away all your negative thought
'video tapes'!
Key Four – It's not me, it's them!
Key Five – Learn to say no!
Key Six – Feed the Light wolf!
Key Seven – Only compare downwards!
Key Eight – Notice the 'mole-hills'!
Key Nine – It could be a lot worse!
Key Ten – Be true to yourself.

CHAPTER EIGHT

Circles of Light

The last chapter was quite heavy going, even for Lightworkers!

Love and **Light** are the **key words** that are the answer to all the questions we can imagine and the lessons which we need to learn.

So obvious, and so much used…we sometimes end our letters with the words 'In Love and Light.'

Under our noses the whole time.

The mysteries will be revealed to us with these words…and so beautifully simple.

Simple words indeed but with hard lessons for us to learn.

The Ten Keys of Love give us the master-key to unlock and release the Light into the world.

We are individual Circles of Light becoming illuminated and shining out to be counted as another soul ready for the days of Heaven on Earth which are coming ever nearer.

Believe in yourself and miracles can happen.

You are a Circle of Light.

A beautiful thought is to imagine yourself as a circle of light surrounded by a ring of unicorns shining a radiant beam of brightness around you in an outer circle of light.

Two Circles of Light, connected but separate and each symbolising completion, unification, integration, illumination and the immortality of the soul.

Hopefully, the previous chapters have helped you on your path to illumination in the following ways:

- By creating your own sacred space and personal place of inner peace
- presented you to the powerful 'twins' of Love and Light
- helped you towards the purification of your emerging soul
- shown you how to protect your spiritual energies
- introduced you to your power animals
- promoted your own self-healing and chakra balancing
- given you the 'keys' to unlock your own highest and most pure potential
- helped you to discover more about the history and heritage of the unicorns, and how to bring their power and magical healing into your everyday life
- Last, but definitely not least, hopefully you have made your own very special unicorn friend!

The unicorns are the Light of the world and bring us to illumination of our soul and the truth of who we are.

Any remaining illusions will be taken away, removed and the mists cleared to reveal the Truth.

The Truth will set you free.

No more restrictions or restricting yourself or others but the FREEDOM TO BE YOURSELF.

Shine your Light in Truth.

No more transformation, but accepting the Truth of who we are NOW.

Maybe this is as good as it gets on this Earth plane of ours.

Accept the shadows and scars on your soul.

Embrace them, they are YOURS!

In the midst of the winds of change STAND STILL and STRONG in the TRUTH of who you are.

Let the Light of Truth shine on your beautiful soul, a circle of Light, and help you on this last stage of unification and integration of your spiritual journey.

Time now to let the Truth set you free

Time now to stand still and strong in the truth of who you are

Time now to accept the shadows and scars of your psyche

And integrate them into your soul,

They are yours.

As the great Rumi said:

'The honey is worth the sting.'

Are you ready to fly with the unicorns?

I really think that you are.

You have your passport to the stars!

The sky is not the limit; you can go above and beyond your wildest dreams and exceed your highest expectations.

There is *no* limit to what you can achieve and you can create your world.

These chapters have taken us on a wonderful healing journey together and now we're ready to fly.

We have met our unicorn helpers, our angel supporters, our power animals, our spirit guides, our ancestor friends and the Ascended Masters.

They are all showering us with unconditional love and the most beautiful brilliant light.

Hopefully, we have had some 'light-bulb' moments when we have seen the light and equally powerfully we have acknowledged and embraced the shadows of our soul. We can now integrate all aspects of our soul, the light, the dark and the in-between, in a beautiful mixture of acceptance, wisdom, serenity and self-knowledge.

We each have many different facets to our whole being.

Time now to bring them all together, not think of ourselves in separate pieces, such as; wife, mother, taxi-driver, healer, writer, cook, nurse, actress, clown, lover, judge, victim, abuser, saboteur, child, addict, angel, artist, bully, father and goddess but, instead, as a **whole** and **integrated** beautiful being.

Now that we can accept ourselves, love ourselves and believe in ourselves we can expect miracles to happen.

We can live the life that we were born to live and fulfil our greatest potential.

The challenges that we may face are our golden opportunities to learn, change and become more self-aware, understanding and wise.

'Know that the rainbow follows the storm.' and
'The gifts of the soul are presents for life.'

We are blessed to meet our spiritual friends along our path. Sometimes we recognise these people, they seem to know us and we them, their eyes really 'see' us.

There is a beautiful ancient Sanskrit word, still used as a greeting, which is **namaste**.

I read a wonderful translation of this very old spiritual word,

'The Light of God in me recognises and honours the Light of God in you and in that recognition is our oneness.'

You are truly blessed when you meet like-minded souls to share your journey.

As my car keyring reminds me, with a Turkish proverb:

'No road is long with good company.'

When we have the weight and support of the Angelic Kingdom walking and flying alongside us we are blessed indeed!

The angels who have introduced themselves to me specifically for this stage of our spiritual development are the Alighting Angels.

They hover above us and then alight on us gently, landing with a graceful unfurling of their magnificent wings like a magical heavenly butterfly. They bring us serenity, grace and most importantly ignite our inner flame with the Divine fire of the eternal spirit.

This spark of pure energy and strength burns with an intensity of a golden-white furnace of warmth and the life-force of the power of good.

This is the spiritual process of Divine magic and alchemy which welds the light of your soul with the fire of spirit to produce your integrated and completed soul.

You are then ready to patiently wait for other souls to become Circles of Light and the days of Heaven on Earth to return.

The Archangel Uriel works with this amazing Light, and oversees this glorious band of angel butterflies as they illuminate and fan the flame of our awakening soul.

We then embrace the Light and Fire of God, and the Universal Life-force to become Divine Torches to shine out into the world for all to see, to choose and then hopefully to follow.

The Alighting Angels have some pretty amazing method of transport.

Can you guess?

The Sacred Winged Unicorns not only carry the angels but bring along their own special blend of power and purity into your life at this auspicious time.

Time now to stand up and be counted as an illuminated soul, a Circle of Light.

Time to help lift the energies of the planet for the glorious days of Heaven on Earth to dawn once again.

Time to be patient and wait awhile for other souls to complete their own integration and completion.

They won't be far behind.

You can continue to shine your Divine Torch out into the world.

A heavenly message from the powers that be!

'Know that you have made a difference and the
Heavens applaud you.
  Know that when enough Circles of Light are shining
  The Earth will spin again and turn into a new cycle
  Of Peace and Harmony for all mankind.
  The Dawning of the New World.
  Know that when the number of souls ready
  To stand up and be counted
  Reach the Divine total of completion
  Then the integration will begin,
  Ascension to the next dimension,
  For those Circles of Light to reach the stars and the
heavens.
  Know that this world that awaits, defies description,
  The Angelic Kingdom of angels, archangels and unicorns,
  The Ascended Masters, the power animals,
  The ancestors, the guides, healers and teachers
  From the beginning of time
  Awake now, to welcome the Circle of Light
  YOU.
  Know that the mysteries will be revealed,
  The answers to all the eternal questions
  Will be given,
  The power and the glory of this beautiful Heaven on
Earth
  Are getting ever closer,
  The days are numbered now,
  YOU are ready to be counted
  As a complete Circle of Light.'

EXERCISE EIGHT

The Light of Truth

This last spiritual exercise brings together and integrates all the different sections of the book.

You will have a sacred space, real or imagined, that you can create or visualise.

You have the support of the heavy gang of Lightworkers.

You are an illuminated soul... a Circle of Light.

Now, as the end is in sight, we are going to reconnect with your unicorn, or lots of new ones.

Please remember to keep in contact with the magical unicorns long after you have read this book.

Remember to expect the unexpected when the unicorns are in your life!

Time to bring down The Light of Truth.

All will become clear.

You can open your eyes to the world, lift the 'veil' and see the Light!

MAGIC!

Now it's time to take yourself to your sacred space.

Prepare the space, in your own way and begin to relax.

Remember that the unicorns are the ULTIMATE beings of Light, power, purity and Master-healing.

Ask them to join with you now...in their multitudes maybe, for the grand finale of this last chapter!

We ask Archangel Uriel to shine his glorious golden-white light on us and all around us to illuminate the path for all the winged unicorns to follow to find us and join with our soul.

Ask your guardian angel to help you accept this wonderful gift of Light.

Breathe in this beautiful light and feel it permeate around your body.

If any part of you is tired or weary, or recovering from disease or illness, or is out of balance or out of sorts in any way let this healing light bring comfort and release from pain.

Breathe the light deeply into your soul and feel surrounded by this healing golden-white light.

Now in the midst of this enveloping light you see your own magnificent unicorns come to join with you at this special spiritual time.

If you are happy to do so, connect with your spiritual friends, old and new, and join together once again in Love and Light.

Enjoy the reconnection and the meeting.

If this is a new unicorn, or several, that you haven't met before then take some time now to introduce yourself.

'Know that whether you can see them or not, there is absolutely no doubt whatsoever that the Unicorn Kingdom is by your side.

Now we are going to bring down The Light of Truth.

This is a powerful, but gentle, beam of pure white light.

Above our heads is our SOUL STAR CHAKRA.

We breathe deeply, and slowly, and imagine this

Pure white light coming over our head

And down into our Soul Star chakra

Like a magnificent halo, shining above us.

Now as we continue to relax and

Know that we are safe and secure,

Protected and surrounded with the Love and Light

Of the Angelic Kingdom,

Especially Archangel Uriel, the Alighting Angels,

And the Sacred Winged Unicorns,

And our own special unicorn/s.

We breathe deeply and slowly and imagine this

Pure white light flowing down into our crown chakra.

It brings us the TRUTH of who we are,

It brings us ancient wisdom

From the Divine source of all that is,

It brings us total acceptance of who we are,

Breathe in this Light of Truth.

Take a moment now to connect deeply

With the essence of who you are.

Put your hand on your heart,

Feel your life-force beating inside you,
Know that you are all that you need to be.
Pull the Light of Truth down to your
HEART CHAKRA.
Your soul centre, the home of your soul.
Let the Light of Truth cleanse and purify,
Illuminate and clarify,
And shine its brilliance on your beautiful soul.

The power of your EARTH STAR CHAKRA
Beneath your feet
Keeps you anchored and grounded,
Safe and secure in the arms of Mother Earth.
Bring the Light of Truth
Deeper into your soul, your psyche,
The special, individual and unique part of you.

Know that you are only human,
And in this incarnation,
You have healed, cleansed, purified,
Forgiven, released, and moved on,
And have now reached
This point on your soul-journey
Where it is now
Time to ACCEPT the shadows and scars of your soul,
Time to EMBRACE them, they are YOURS!!
Time to STAND STILL and STRONG in the
TRUTH of who you are.
Breathe in this Light of Love and Light of Truth

And let them shine brightly
Into our inner being.

Know that the Archangels and Sacred Unicorns
Stand beside us, now and always.
Know that they surround us with
Unconditional love, and shower us with the
PEACE of the World to come,
And fill us with the joy and happiness
Which passes all understanding.
Know that they help us to accept and embrace
Our darkness,
And help us to realise that we are
Beings of Pure Light,
And that our shadows help us to heal others,
And bring us closer to God and the angels
Who understand and accept us and embrace us
Just as we are.

Know that to face up to our own darkness,
And the darkness of others
Without criticism, judgement or condemnation
But with love, acceptance and approval.
To accept the fears and darkness of others
Is the greatest gift
That we can bestow on ourselves and our fellow man.
Time now to shine your Light of Truth
Out into the world.
Time now to become a Torch-bearer

And take your light out into the world,
Time now to shine your light for others to follow,
Time now to shine your light to lead others out of the
darkness,
Time now to shine your light to illuminate the path for
others to find,
Time now to shine your light to heal and inspire
others,
Time now to shine your light to show others the way
forward closer to their
Own illumination,
YOU are a being of LIGHT,
Time to SHINE...

Now it is time to thank our supporters, guides, our angels and our unicorns and everyone else that has helped and encouraged us on our journey today and other days.

Open your eyes, wriggle your fingers and toes, have a shake and come back into reality.

Maybe it's time for writing up your journal.

Definitely time for a cup of tea!

I do hope you have enjoyed bringing the unicorns into your living-room and into your life.

They have certainly adored making your acquaintance.

That's Omega's grand and majestic turn of phrase.

He's asking *me* to end on a high note!

So here's a high E from me...!

And the very last words have to be given to our

fabulous friend, Omega, who wants me to tell you again that he represents the brains, beauty, wisdom, power and glory of the Unicorn Kingdom!

'The great and wonderful souls that have been,
That are and that will be,
Have all walked and journeyed the same path,
The road to find themselves,
To touch their soul,
To find the unconditional love,
For themselves,
It has been my pleasure and privilege
To play a small, but important part of this
Spiritual journey of YOURS,
I hope you have enjoyed the ride so far!
I'm here now with all my
Fabulous friends
From the Angelic Kingdom and beyond,
And will be with YOU
Now and always,
In all ways
God Speed!'

This is not the end, but a beginning!

Ascension to the Fifth Dimension and Heaven on Earth is just around the corner...

After a successful management career in the ceramic industry, Adela Simons now works as a spiritual healer, teacher and writer. She also runs workshops, gives talks and leads meditation groups. These focus on healing and the Angelic Kingdom of angels, archangels and unicorns. Adela is now a human signpost for many of those on their spiritual and soul journeys.

If you would like to write to her she is very happy to hear from you by email at: adelasimons@gmail.com

Notes

A UNICORN IN YOUR LIVING-ROOM

A UNICORN IN YOUR LIVING-ROOM

Notes